ON EDITORIALIZATION
STRUCTURING SPACE
AND AUTHORITY
IN THE DIGITAL AGE
MARCELLO
VITALI-ROSATI

Theory on Demand #26
On Editorialization: Structuring Space and Authority in the Digital Age

Author: Marcello Vitali-Rosati
Editor: Miriam Rasch
Cover design: Katja van Stiphout
Design: Rosie Underwood
EPUB development: Rosie Underwood
Published by the Institute of Network Cultures, Amsterdam, 2018
ISBN: 978-94-92302-20-5

The research was supported by Le Fonds de recherche du Québec – Société et culture and Social Sciences and Humanities Research Council of Canada.

Contact
Institute of Network Cultures
Phone: +3120 5951865
Email: info@networkcultures.org
Web: http://www.networkcultures.org

This publication is available through various print on demand services and freely downloadable from http://networkcultures.org/publications

CONTENTS

to ariane and hélène

ACKNOWLEDGMENTS

This book presents the results of a research realized within the Canada Research Chair on digital textualities (http://digitaltextualities.ca), financed by the Social Sciences and Humanities Research Council of Canada and by Le Fonds de recherche du Québec – Société et culture.

Nobody thinks alone: the ideas presented in this book are the result of many years of discussions and collaborative work. In many ways, I am not the author of them. A special thank goes to Enrico Agostini-Marchese, Peppe Cavallari, Emmanuel Château-Dutier, Jean-Claude Guédon, Jean-Marc Larrue, Louise Merzeau, Servanne Monjour, Michael Nardone, Élisabeth Routhier, Nicolas Sauret, Michael Sinatra, Matteo Treleani, Gérard Wormser – for their help, their suggestions, their ideas, their time and their friendship.

To think means to look for a word... my words and my sentences have been revised by Robert Rose and Miriam Rasch: I thank them for their generosity in trying to understand my text and in making it better.

1. A CONCLUSION AS AN INTRODUCTION

Main Thesis

Writing a book, like reading one, is a journey. And when we embark on a journey, a map can be useful. This is why I propose in this introduction to offer something that is usually found in a conclusion: the set of results that will be presented in the book. Reading a map is not the same as making the journey, of course, but it can help to complete it and it can also give a pretty good idea of what will be found on the journey. Sometimes the map is enough and we may decide not to make the journey at all.

This book is about authority in digital space. The main thesis of the book is that digital space is a structured space with its own characteristics and its own specific forms of authority. A corollary of this thesis is that, like every other space, digital space is a frame and a context for actions: it carries values and it shapes and influences actions. In this sense, studying digital space and revealing its structures is necessary to understanding the conditions of possibility for politics in the digital age.

However, the notion that the structures of digital space shape actions by setting a particular political framework does not imply that digital space is intrinsically characterized by a particular political orientation. In other words, it is important to avoid the fundamental antinomy that so often characterizes the mass media's discourse about digital technologies: one set of voices asserts confidently that digital technologies make us freer; another set tells us that digital technologies make us less free.

Both these statements are defensible and to some extent both are true. Moreover, both have contradictory symmetrical counterparts. The positive argument, according to which digital technologies make us freer, has some obvious affinity with the negative position that sees no possibility for organization in the digital environment and is convinced that the digital age is leading to anarchy (with anarchy here intended as a bad thing). The negative argument, on the other hand, according to which digital technologies reduce freedom, can be tied to the positive notion that digital technologies give us more power to control and organize the world (with power here intended as a good thing).

The fact that these two statements with contradictory moral implications can be defended forces us to recognize that we should separate moral judgment from structural analysis. In the following pages, we will examine how digital space is structured and how these struc-tures influence human actions. We will conduct an analysis of the political stakes involved and the power dynamics at work in the age of digital technologies. This analysis will allow us to identify how our practices can influence politics today. In other words, this book wants to continue in the tradition of 'net criticism' initiated by Geert Lovink. According to Lovink, 'Net criticism is a call for critical intellectual engagement. It is not a critique of information or technology in general.'[1]

---

1   Geert Lovink, *My First Recession: Critical Internet Culture in Transition,* Rotterdam: V2_NAi Publishers, 2003, p. 9.

Complementary Thesis and Definitions

The main thesis of the book is supported by other important theses and definitions:

Definition 1: Authority is something we trust without being rationally convinced or compelled by violence. Authority should not be confused with power. Authority can – and often does – generate power, but not every power is based on authority. This definition – which is the one given by Hannah Arendt[2] – implies that authority is not only necessary but also what limits the reach of powers: totalitarian power results from a lack of authority, which actuates the necessity of violence.

Definition 2: A space is a particular dynamic set of relationships between objects. These relationships can be of different kinds, including of distance, visibility, and position. Structuring a relationship between objects also means determining certain values: the fact that something is more visible than something else, for example, implies that the former is more important than the latter. For this reason, a space always carries values. The relationships are always something written, and there is a deep link between inhabiting a space, reading it, and writing it.

Thesis 1: Each authority is the result of a particular spatial structure. A space is a configuration that generates the possibility of trust. Trust is the result of the particular structure of the relationships between objects. Changing space means also changing the kind of authority we can trust.

Definition 3: Digital space is the space where we live. It is the set of relationships between a hybridization of connected and non-connected objects. The adjective 'digital' must be considered as a qualification of time or period: there is modern space, contemporary space, and then digital space. Digital space is the space of today's societies.

Thesis 2: Digital space is a well-structured material space. We should not consider digital space as immaterial or as something without a given structure. It is true that digital space is dynamic, but this is true of any space because every space is in motion. The structure of digital space is produced by what we call 'editorialization'.

Definition 4: Editorialization is the set of dynamics that produce and structure digital space. These dynamics can be understood as the interactions of individual and collective actions within a particular digital environment.

Thesis 3: Digital space has its own forms of authority. This thesis is the logical consequence of the third definition and the first thesis. Digital space is, moreover a space full of authorities, which means that it is a space characterized by a high level of trust.

---

2   Hannah Arendt, *Between Past and Future: Eight Exercises in Political Thought,* New York: Penguin Books, 2006.

Thesis 4: Authorities in digital space are shaped by the characteristics of editorialization. We can summarize these characteristics as follows:

- Authorities are processual. Digital authorities legitimate a process and not particular information. The processual nature of digital authorities is related to the progressive disappearing of the notion of originality, which is due to the intrinsic multiplicity of digital objects.

- Authorities are performative: they produce themselves. Authority is thus proportional to activity.

- Authorities are non-representational. Authority cannot be interpreted using a truth-based model. Authority does not guarantee that content – whether a sentence or any other piece of information – corresponds to reality: authority is what creates reality.

- Authorities are multiple. Digital space is characterized by the coexistence of many authorities, which can differ a lot from each other and often are contradictory. This multiplicity also leads to the coexistence, in digital space, of pre-digital and digital-native authorities.

- Authorities are collective. The emergence of authorities always depends on collective interactions.

The Path of the Book

The definitions and theses above will be discussed and explained in the first three chapters of the book. The first chapter ('The Crisis of Authority') will show how the changes produced by digital technologies have led to a crisis for some pre-digital forms of authority. In this chapter we will offer a definition of authority and space (definitions 1 and 2), and discuss the thesis according to which authority depends on a particular structure of space (thesis 1). In the second chapter ('The Structure of the Digital') we will analyze the meaning of the word 'digital' in order to arrive at a definition of digital space (definition 3). We will show that digital space is a well-structured material space, with its own values and characteristics (thesis 2). These characteristics depend on what we call 'editorialization'. In the third chapter ('Editorialization') we will give a definition of 'editorialization' (definition 4) and analyze the characteristics of editorialization. Using this analysis, we will identify the forms of authority that characterize digital space (thesis 3 and 4).

The theses demonstrated in the first three chapters pose two main problems. The first is the difficulty of finding a way to critically interpret authority in digital space. Authority must be questioned. This is crucial because an unquestionable authority easily becomes a violent power. Trust in an authority should always be accompanied by a willingness and ability to criticize and question it. More accurately, we might say that the aim should not be to determine whether (or why) an authority is reliable but rather to figure out where it is reliable. In fact, it is not really possible to decide if or why an authority is reliable because this would mean that we are able to identify some political or ethical principle that is valid in a universal way, independent of any particular space. Political values are inseparable from the organization of the space, however. A critical awareness does not give us the ability to understand the rationality of an authority. There is no rational argument for trusting an authority because of the very definition of authority; we can only understand its reach and identify its perimeters. Still, this understanding is the basis of the possibility of freedom: it allows us to possess the knowledge that what we trust in one context – in one space – is not valid elsewhere, in another space. No authority is absolute; it is always relative to some ethical or political frame that is specific to a particular space. The problem with digital authorities is that the relatively new structure of the space makes it difficult to understand them.

The second problematic aspect is understanding digital authorities' relationships with the private and the public spheres. If authority depends on space, it is crucial to know how this space is produced and whether it can be considered a public space or not. In other words: are digital authorities private or public authorities? The last chapter of this book ('Writing Public Space') will propose an analysis of these political stakes and offer perspectives on how to face these problems.

Methodology

In this book 'the digital' is considered in the continuity of a longstanding philosophical tradition; the changes the digital has produced are analyzed not as a break but as the continuation of certain conceptual structures that can be found in the history of Western philosophy. The digital therefore is seen not as a set of tools, but rather as a culture in its own right that now shapes our views of the world, our interpretations of reality and, foremost, our political practices. What is politics in the digital age? What are the stakes of our actions today? How do we consider freedom? These are questions that the book tries to answer. The digital is not the object of this book; it is simply the adjective that that we use to define our contemporary practices as a whole. A philosophical reflection cannot be legitimate today unless it takes into account the cultural characteristics of digital society.

2. THE CRISIS OF AUTHORITY

On 31 October 1517, Martin Luther posted his famous *Ninety-Five Theses* on the door of the Castle Church of Wittenberg. Luther's text aimed to question the validity of selling indulgences. In the view of the Augustinian monk, the Pope did not have the authority to remit the punishment of sins. In the fifth thesis Luther writes:

> The pope does not intend to remit and cannot remit any penalties other than those which he has imposed either by his own authority or by that of the Canons (*arbitrio vel suo vel canonum*).[3]

The authority of the Pope, Luther insisted, was not the same as the authority of God: the Pope had power only over the penalties he himself had established. Luther continues in the sixth thesis:

> The pope cannot remit any guilt, except by declaring that it has been remitted by God and by assenting to God's remission; though, to be sure, he may grant remission in cases reserved to his judgment. If his right to grant remission in such cases were despised, the guilt would remain entirely unforgiven.[4]

What Luther is saying here is that there is a clear difference between God's authority and the will of the Pope. There are, in other words, two distinct forms of authority to consider: a divine one – the one of God – and a temporal one – the one of the Pope. This separation implies a huge revolution in the sense that it leads to the attenuation of temporal authority, something we might call a crisis of known authority. One could go further and say that Pope's authority should no longer be considered as an authority in the proper sense. If we read the original Latin text of the *Ninety-Five Theses,* the term 'authority' is not actually employed. Luther speaks about 'arbitrius' (will) or 'potestas' (power). In the ninetieth thesis he argues:

> To repress these arguments and scruples of the laity by force alone (*sola potestate*) and not to resolve them by giving reasons, is to expose the Church and the pope to the ridicule of their enemies and to make Christians unhappy.[5]

---

3   Martin Luther, 'Disputation of Doctor Martin Luther on the Power and Efficacy of Indulgences', *Wikisource*, https://en.wikisource.org/wiki/Disputation_of_Doctor_Martin_Luther_on_the_Power_and_Efficacy_of_ Indulgences. The original Latin text is: 'Papa non vult nec potest ullas poenas remittere: praeter eas, quas arbitrio vel suo vel canonum imposuit.' See: 'Disputatio pro Declaratione Virtutis Indulgentiarum – Wikisource', https://la.wikisource.org/wiki/Disputatio_pro_declaratione_virtutis_indulgentiarum.

4   See: 'Disputatio'. The original Latin text is: 'Papa non potest remittere ullam culpam, nisi declarando et approbando remissam a deo. Aut certe remittendo casus reservatos sibi, quibus contemptis culpa prorsus remaneret.'

5   See: 'Disputatio'. The Latin text is: 'Hec scrupulosissima laicorum argumenta sola potestate compescere nec reddita ratione diluere, Est ecclesiam et Papam hostibus ridendos exponere et infelices christianos facere.'

On one hand, there is the will of the Pope and of the Church and their power to make people respect it. On the other hand, there is the authority of God, which is clearly something quite different.

The problem raised by such an argument is how to identify God's authority, or, to be more precise, how to identify authority in general, since one cannot speak directly with God to know his will or thought. Another development is deeply linked to this problem and so to Luther's theses: the German translation of the Bible and the possibility of letting religious texts circulate in the wake of the invention of the printing press. God's authority can be found in religious texts, which therefore all Christians have to be able to read. The crisis of temporal authority implies neither a lack of authority nor an end to it. Rather, it determines a shift: authority moves from the Pope to the text. For this to be possible, something else was necessary: the emergence of philology, the science of studying and interpreting a text, which developed in relationship to the growing circulation of texts as caused by invention of the printing press.

Five hundred years later, we face an analogous crisis of authority. And once again, the crisis does not mean the disappearance of all authority. It means instead that authority has shifted from one realm to another. This book attempts to identify this shift and to analyze the new forms of authority that are emerging in the digital age.

What Is Authority?

We are all used to authority of some kind. We encounter authority first as children, in the form of parental authority. Later we are introduced to the authority of teachers and, later still, to the authority of the State, the most visible expressions of which are the laws that we must learn to respect. For some, religion exerts authority, through texts or through the Church or through other institutions. But these are not the only forms of authority that are present in contemporary western societies. One of the most important forms of authority that we learn to identify and to respect is the authority of authors. This is the authority of what has been written by someone who knows more than someone else about a particular subject.

This form of authority manifests itself in a number of different ways. It may be simply the authority of someone who has learned something – by studying or by practicing a specific discipline. Specialized knowledge underpins the authority of a medical doctor, or of a lawyer, or of a carpenter: in these cases, authority is issued by competence. And behind the competence there is always some function, which further strengthens authority: a doctor knows how to cure a disease because somebody – an author – has invented or experimented with a drug or some other kind of care. One might object that, in the case of a more manual art – like carpentry – it does not work quite in this way, because there is no need of an author in the strictest sense of the term. A carpenter can learn the secrets of his art simply by observing a more experienced carpenter. If the term 'author' is used in a wider sense, however, it becomes clear that even in the case of manual arts where mastery is typically achieved through a combination of oral transmission and practical apprenticeship, there is an original, authorial figure – someone, for instance, who invented or experimented with a particular technique to work the wood. In contemporary society, the learning of an art – even the most manual – almost always has to pass throughout some text. The realm of science presents yet another example of the authority of an author: we trust the principles and the predictions of science because we trust the scientists who, thanks to their study and their knowledge, have written them.

These examples help us to identify a fundamental characteristic of authority: it is something we trust. As small children, we trust our parents; we think that what they say is true, that they are able to guide us because they know the world and how it works. It is important to point out, though, that in these examples authority is not the same as power. Parents have the *power* to decide for children and to impose on them ways of behaving and conducting themselves, but this is not the source of their authority. *Authority*, as it is understood here, stems from the fact that children trust their parents because they believe their parents are right. The same difference can be pointed out in the case of the State's authority: states have the power to make people obey laws, but this power is not enough to make a society. Citizens must believe that laws are fair, that they are based on some true principle. Citizens must *trust* the State. In the case of the authority of a teacher or a medical doctor, the difference between authority and power is even more evident. A medical doctor does not have the power to impose care on patients. A patient listens to a doctor only if and because they trusts them.

But why do we trust an authority? How does an authority become an authority? And, we may ask, when does an authority *stop* being an authority? The way we understand and produce authority is of particular importance at this moment, because these processes are undergoing a dramatic change as a result of the internet – or more precisely the web. Two distinct strands of discourse have tried to make sense of this change: one points to the idea that the internet has allowed (or has not allowed) us to be freer, while the other stresses the notion that the internet has lead to a loss of institutional control.

The origin of the first kind of statement – the internet gives us freedom – can be traced to the origins of internet and its development during the 1970s.[6] A mix of different ideologies and approaches initially inspired the development of the internet. On one hand, there was a need to find a valuable solution for military communications in case of war. Arpanet, for example, was a military project. On the other hand, there was the hippie movement and the idea that technology could improve our freedom, especially by multiplying access to documents and thus to knowledge. This was the idea of the Computer Liberation Front. This kind of argument is still present today, though it is represented more in the public discourse of some media or online communities than in the work of scholars. It can be heard in the rhetoric of the cyber-libertarian movement – the Technology Liberation Front is an example.[7] The basic idea is that the internet improves freedom of expression and destroys any limitations put on such freedoms by the ancient model of top-down communication. Big institutions, like national newspapers or television, cannot monopolize communication anymore: online, everybody can express themselves as they wants. The circulation of content, opinions, and information no longer has

---

6   See for example Dominique Cardon, *La démocratie internet: promesses et limites*, Paris: Seuil, 2010.
7   See, http://techliberation.com/.

boundaries or limits. As many scholars have pointed out,[8] however, there is only a very small number of elite blogs that are actually read online, and the idea that everyone has the same importance and the same audience as a traditional newspaper is only a myth.

An important dimension of this debate about freedom and the internet is the impact that the network has on democracy. The debate has become particularly intense in the wake of the Arab Spring, especially with respect to the question of whether new technologies – specifically the participatory web and social networks – provide people with more opportunities to be active in politics and thus improve democracy. Peter Dahlgren,[9] for one, analyzing specific cases like the revolt in Slovenia and the Occupy Wall Street movement, has concluded that the web has indeed provided some alternative forms of democratic participation. His thesis is that the web has created opportunities to circumvent traditional electoral politics and so has improved the democratic process. Evgeny Morozov in contrast, insists that the idea that the web has improved freedom and democracy is a myth propagated by 'Silicon Valley ideology'.[10] Instead of giving people more freedom, the web has in fact produced many control structures that are owned and managed by a small number of private corporations. The network thus threatens the democracy.

As Henry Farrell points out,[11] though, it is difficult to decide which of these positions is most persuasive because the meanings of the political ideas employed – democracy, freedom – are far from clear. To some extent, we can agree with the thesis that the web has given more tools to people and has improved freedom of expression and communication; but, in some cases, it has given more control tools to institutions – both public or private – which use these tools to reduce people's freedoms. This has been the case in China, for instance, as Rebecca MacKinnon has shown.[12] In order to decide if the network is giving us more or less freedom, it is therefore necessary to understand what is meant by terms such as 'freedom' and 'democracy'. But it is impossible to come up with any clear definitions if we do not first understand how society is changed by the network. For this reason, the relationship between the internet and freedom will not be the primary focus in this book.

More relevant to the discussion here is the second strand of discourse mentioned earlier, the one that concerns itself with the ways in which new forms of production and the circulation of content and information on the network have set in motion a crisis in the institutions that formerly managed this production and this circulation. The centers of power that we used to know are in some sort of a crisis; they are losing the control they once had. This does not

---

8   See for example, Clay Shirky, 'Shirky: Power Laws, Weblogs and Inequality', 8 February 2003, http://www.shirky.com/writings/powerlaw_weblog.html; Henry Farrell and Daniel W. Drezner, 'The Power and Politics of Blogs', *Public Choice* 134, no. 1-2 (2007): 15-30, doi:10.1007/s11127-007-9198-1.

9   Peter Dahlgren, *The Political Web: Media, Participation and Alternative Democracy*, London: Palgrave Macmillan, 2013.

10 See Evgeny Morozov, *The Net Delusion: The Dark Side of Internet Freedom*, New York: PublicAffairs, 2012.

11 Henry Farrell, 'The Consequences of the Internet for Politics', *Annual Review of Political Science* 15.1 (2012): 35-52, doi:10.1146/annurev-polisci-030810-110815.

12 Rebecca MacKinnon, *Consent of the Networked: The Worldwide Struggle for Internet Freedom*, Basic Books, 2012.

mean that there is no control anymore, only that it is not in the same hands – not the same institutions, not the same actors. Saskia Sassen has underlined this crisis of modern centers of power many times in her work.[13]

What is of particular interest here is the fact that the centers of power that are currently experiencing a crisis are the same ones that were created and organized at the time of the invention of the printing press: that is, when Luther posted his *Ninety-Five Theses* on the Wittenberg Cathedral's door. The change of the model of production and circulation of contents, it would seem, leads to a transformation of the way we understand authority. And this transformation implies a reconfiguration of the mechanisms of power. The internet is not producing a political revolution; it is only modifying our ways of dealing with knowledge. But this modification does have the effect that the sources of authority do not stay the same and so we do not trust the same institutions anymore; nor do we grant them the same influence or the same power that they had before.

The example of Wikipedia offers a good illustration of this situation of crisis. In addition to being one of the most visited websites in the world, Wikipedia is also one of the most important sources of information for the average web surfer. This in itself indicates that Wikipedia has become an authority of sorts. The fact that millions of web surfers seek for information on Wikipedia suggests that they trust it, that they have granted it the status of authority. And this granting of authority to a new source has in turn destabilized other, more traditional forms of authority. An example is how formerly, during a university lecture, the only authority that was recognized was the one of the professor. They were the specialist who had the knowledge, who knew better than anyone the subject they were talking about. Nobody could doubt what they were saying. But today the student can easily verify the accuracy of the information online. The student can consult Wikipedia to see if the professor 'is right'. In other words, the professor will be considered right only if the information they provide corresponds with information found on Wikipedia or other sources deemed authoritative. This means that the professor is no longer the (only) authority on a given subject; that designation has shifted. One could object that before Wikipedia a student could question a professor's authority by consulting a book or a printed encyclopedia. And this is certainly true. But a printed book is not immediately available in a classroom and, more importantly, the authority of a book is based on the same model as the professor's authority: it is an *authorial* authority. Wikipedia offers something quite different: a new model of authority, one that departs from the models that we used to know until ten or twenty years ago.

Another example is the impact of online health forums and other online health information sources on the authority of health professionals. As many scholars have observed,[14] the use of the internet for health information is becoming more and more frequent. Gualtieri and Pratt even speak of 'Dr.

---

13   See, for example, Saskia Sassen, *Losing Control?: Sovereignty in the Age of Globalization*, New York: Columbia University Press, 2014.

14   Gul Seckin, 'Health Information on the Web and Consumers' Perspectives on Health Professionals' Responses to Information Exchange', *Medicine 2.0* 3.2 (2014), doi:10.2196/med20.3213.

Google',[15] pointing out that almost every patient conducts some online research on their problem and often tries to make a diagnosis themselves, thus questioning the doctor's authority from the start. Before the existence of the web, it took a lot of effort for a patient to gather information about their disease. In order to do so, they had to go to a specialized library and read academic papers that were difficult for a layperson to understand. They might find a popularized book, but it would probably be expensive, and its trustworthiness would not be easy to identify. The authority of the health professional was thus based in large part on the fact that they were the only one who had access to, or could even understand, information about a specific disease or ailment. The quantity, as well as the accessibility, of online information on medical conditions thus has changed the ways that doctors are perceived as authorities. The authority of a doctor can no longer be attributed to a privileged access to information. In this respect, the crisis that the authority of the medical professional now faces, is highly similar to the crisis that emerged in the time of Luther: the possibility of printing and then circulating many copies of the Bible created a situation in which people no longer needed the mediation of the Church – and so the Church lost its authority. These examples reveal an important relationship between authority and knowledge, but it is one that is changing. In the case of Wikipedia, access to information has made it possible to know something that used to be known only by a specialist. The same can be said of online health information. The access to knowledge is definitely an important element for authority, but it is not the only one. Knowledge has to do with trust and trust can be gained in other ways than only through the possession of specialized knowledge. If authority is something we trust, the question is: why do we trust it? How does an authority become something that we put our trust in?

One way to answer these questions is to examine the etymological origins of the word *authority*. It comes from the Latin verb *augere*, which means 'to augment'. From the same etymological root comes the word *author*. An authority is an entity that augments something. One could say that an authority augments the weight of something, its importance. An authority adds weight to an object and makes it reliable. In the same sense, an author augments the weight of information or content by giving it reliability. Thus authority is not only based on the access to knowledge, but also on the possibility of making this knowledge reliable and legitimate it. This is the function of an authority: after an augmentation made by an authority, an object acquires its legitimacy, it is more important, it is reliable. The augmentation made by the authority thus produces trust. But how can the authority do this?

The clearest form of augmentation produced by an authority is the 'ipse dixit', the formula used in scholastic texts to give credibility to a sentence. 'Ipse dixit' means: he, himself, said this. An author said this. In the Middle Ages, an author was only a figure from antiquity, someone who had an absolute authority. Aristotle was considered the most prominent author and the formula 'ipse dixit' was often used in reference to him. Because Aristotle said this, it must be true. Aristotle is the *author* – the authority – who augmented the importance of a sentence by giving it an absolute reliability. The name 'Aristotle' was like a certificate of truth, like a stamp on a document that guarantees its authenticity.

---

15   Lisa Neal Gualtieri and Janey Pratt, 'Dr. Google', *Magazine of the Tufts University Medical and Sackler Alumni Association* 68, no. 1 (2009): 14-18.

If we analyze the examples of the teacher and the doctor, we can identify the same structure: a piece of information is true because the teacher gives it. The teacher is thus a function of legitimation. A student can say, 'the teacher said this', in order to prove the truth of an affirmation. Likewise, a patient can use the expression 'the doctor said this' as an equivalent to 'this information is true'. Once again, authority in these cases is not based on power. A student does not think that the teacher tells the truth because of her or his power. A patient is not forced by a power to recognize the doctor's authority. On the contrary, the power of teachers and doctors depends on their authority; it is generated by it. Hannah Arendt explains that authority is something we obey without being forced to. An authority is something we trust without power. Authority, says Arendt,[16] is incompatible with constriction and persuasion. We trust an authority without being forced to and without any argumentation. The affirmation 'the teacher said it' does not need any further explanation: we do not need to explain why what the teacher said is true; it is true just because the teacher said it. Our question remains unanswered, though: where does authority come from? How can an authority add legitimacy to information, to content?

A Particular Structure of Space

The hypothesis I would like to propose is that *authority is possible only because of a particular structure of space*. The function of adding legitimacy and reliability to an object or to content depends on the fact that we are in a space which has a clear structure, that is easy to identify and to understand. It is through an analysis of this structure that we can begin to figure out how authority works and why we trust it. If a given authority is deeply linked to the structure of a space, we cannot consider it as absolute. The authority does not work everywhere; it is thus regional. Some examples support this thesis. Let us consider the case of the parent's authority, the one of the doctor's authority, the case of the religious authority and, finally, the one of the book's authority.

Parental authority is clearly linked with the space of the house. It is a domestic authority; the boundaries of it are very stable and the child is always able to recognize them. What is said by parents is reliable because we are at home. Every principle is based on this space and on the possibility of understanding when one is in it and when one is out of it. As an example, the rule that one must go to bed at 8pm can be a legitimate obligation, based on a theoretical principle – which is not always explicit but always implicitly shared by parents and children. The principle could be something like: 'going to sleep at 8pm is necessary for the well-being of a child'. Or 'a child must sleep ten hours' each night. This principle is guaranteed by the authority of the parents: the child trusts the principle because it comes from them. But this trust is not absolute: the child is able to relativize it according to the space where they are. When they are elsewhere – for instance at their grandparent's – they are open to trust another principle, even if it appears deeply different or contradictory. For example it would be acceptable to go to bed later, to eat differently, to respect silence when grandpa is reading his newspaper and so on. So, the authority of the parents is completely valid at home, but it has a limited impact elsewhere. This limitation at the same time makes it possible to understand

---

16   Arendt, *Between Past and Future*, p. 92.

the authorial principle and to relativize it. This means that the production of authority depends on a specific organization of objects, actions and rules. The principle 'going to sleep at 8pm is necessary for the well-being of a child' is true only because of a particular organization of the domestic universe.

The case of the doctor's authority is more complex, because it appears to be a universal authority, without boundaries. This is because of the universality which characterizes the discourse of western science. But if we analyze the situation more attentively we can easily see that this universality is actually localized and that the reliability of a doctor – and thus their authority – is also deeply linked to a specific organization of space. First of all, there is a process of credentialization that depends on the education system of a specific country. One can trust a doctor, first of all, because they are a doctor, which means that they have graduated from a specific program. This graduation is recognized only in the very country where it is achieved. If the doctor has Italian credentials and they want to practice in Canada, they must make their studies recognized in Canada; otherwise they are not actually a doctor in Canada. The authority of the doctor is based on a national system and is valuable only within this particular space. One might add that there are other localizations – like a particular idea of what medicine should be – which also depends on a cultural system characterizing a specific territory.

These first two examples make clear that the space we are referring to as the basis of every authority is not only a territory but also a symbolic space: the space of a discourse, as in the case of western medicine and the domestic organization of daily life, as in the case of the authority of the parents. If we take the example of religion, it is clear that the space on which its authority depends is not – or at least not primarily – a territory, but the space of a particular discourse. The authority of the Gospels is valid only in Christianity, the authority of the Koran only in Islam. For the authority to exist, an act of faith is necessary and such an act involves entering the space of a specific religious discourse. The act of faith means entering a space and accepting its rules and its structures. One can accept the authority of a religious text only thanks to this adhesion: the structure of the discourse implies that a text – or a person – is reliable. Religion, of course, can be based on power rather than authority, when people are forced through the threat of violence to obey religious authority. But in such cases, as Arendt makes clear, we are no longer talking about authority.

Let us consider the last example: the book. A book is a perfect illustration of a clearly organized space. The boundaries of a book are clear: something is in the book, something is out of it. The object-book has its threshold:[17] the cover, the name of the author, the page numbers and all the paratextual elements which make a link between the inner space of the book and what is out of the book. It is because of this clear organization that a book has – or does not have – an authority. Let us consider a specific example of a book, *Remediation: Understanding New Media* by Jay David Bolter and Richard Grusin. I have this object in my hands: why do I trust what I read in this book? Where does the authority of this text come from? I look at the book and I first see its black cover. On this cover I find the names of the two authors and the title. Thanks to an editorial convention, I can easily guess the meaning of this text: I know that the names on the cover are the names of

---

17   Gérard Genette, *Seuils*, Paris: Points Seuil, 2002.

the authors and I know what an author is. The title allows me to understand what kind of book I have in my hands, the graphics of the cover tell me that it is probably an academic book – I am used to the editorial codes. On the spine, I can see the logo of MIT press. When I open the book, I immediately find all the crucial information about this publication on the front matter: the publishing house, the date, the place, the copyright information. I am able to know that this book was first published in 1999. I have a table of contents which explains to me the structure of the book and what topics it treats. All this information structures a particular space: it tells me about the place of the book in the general space of publications: it is an academic book, published by an academic publishing house, which demands a peer review before the publication; it is a book from 1999 – which means that I can locate the discourse of the book in time and space. I can trust what Bolter and Grusin say in the book because they say it in this book, in a particular context of which I know and understand the rules and the structure. Every sentence is valid within this particular context. I can place every sentence in the academic analysis of media which has been developed in a particular tradition of media theory. It is self-evident that any sentence Bolter an Grusin have uttered in a space different from this book – something they may have said during an interview, or something they said during a conference or a private conversation – has not the same reliability. What I trust is thus the structure of a book which is integrated to a more complex structure: the one of a particular publishing model.

Space and Relationships

We will come back to this example. For the moment the question I would like to address is: what exactly do we mean when we speak about 'space'? The word 'space' is used here in a Foucauldian sense (and not in either a Cartesian or a Kantian sense). In his text 'Des espaces autres',[18] Foucault explains that space has been defined variously by *localization* (in the medieval period), by *extension* (during the Renaissance), and by the *site* (*emplacement* in French), which is how it is defined today. In the Middle Ages, space was organized hierarchically. The hierarchy was stable and defined by transcendent forces. Space was the localization of objects in this hierarchy. During the Renaissance this idea changed and space was interpreted in a mathematical way: as a formal extension, a uniform area that could be measured objectively. A space was a set of homogeneous points that could be identified using numbers. This is the Galilean and Cartesian idea of space, which can be represented by three axes. In modern and contemporary society this idea of space has been replaced by the notion of the site, which we can define as a set of relationships between objects.

This is the definition we will use. The way a set of relationships is structured can be understood as its space. Indeed, if a phenomenological interpretation of the notion of space is used,[19] space should not be considered as a stable object – something given and independent from us – but rather as dynamic. The links between the objects are in continuous movement and their layout is a dynamic process. Therefore, we can only speak about a space if we live in it and inhabit it. Crossing the space, occupying it, means producing it: the space is the result of an inhabitation

---

18   Michel Foucault, 'Des espaces autres', *Architecture, Mouvement, Continuité*, no. 5 (1984): 46-49.
19   I refer in particular to Merleau-Ponty's redefinition of space in the *Phénoménologie de la perception*, Paris: Gallimard, 1945.

process. The interpretation of space we proposes here is thus a continuity of the tradition of Lefebvre: space is not something given, but it is the result of a production process.[20]

Let us look at an example in order to explain this idea. One of the relationships of which space is made is the distance between objects.[21] Two objects are more or less close to one another. Although this relationship may appear as given – stable and crystallized – this is actually not the case. For example: what is the distance between Montreal and New York? If we consider space as something that is given, objective and immutable, we will think that we can measure this distance and have only one answer. I can look for this data by searching on Google maps and find a specific distance: 376 miles. However, this data is far from objective. It indicates the distance from Montreal to New York if we take a particular road. If I take another road, the distance is 371 miles – but the trip will be longer. I can calculate this distance in many different ways, according to the reason why I am looking for it. I can easily grasp that the distance depends on the way I want to traverse it. Montreal is close to New York if I have a car, but it is closer if I go there by plane, farther if I take the train and very far if I want to reach it by walking. There are many other factors that one can cite: the traffic, the price of fuel, the price of flights, the hours of the flights. There is also the fact that New York is well-known to Montrealers – which, naturally, makes it closer psychically. Hence, in order to know the distance between two objects one has to traverse it, or at least know how to plan to traverse it.

The space between two places can thus be seen as a set of relationships that are dynamic because they unfold and are created only as the distance is traversed: an objective relationship does not exist, because each relationship is the issue of a specific action. This is what I mean when I say that a space exists as we inhabit it. The idea of an objective space is abstract and empty. One could reply that there is in fact an objective distance, even if we can traverse it in different ways. It would be the distance measured along a straight line. But even this is nothing more than another way of traversing a distance: in order to have the very concept of distance in a straight line, we must invent the principle of a map, the idea of Mercator's projection, and so on. Or, if we want a simpler solution, we could imagine a crow traversing the distance: this is why the distance in a straight line is a distance as the crow flies. Still, this is also a way of imagining how the space can be traversed and is not objective in any way. Space is thus always the result of a production process. This principle is valid for every relationship that creates a given space. Or, to put it in slightly different terms: every space is a particular way of creating relationships between objects. It will be useful to consider some familiar examples; three spaces that we are all used to and that have varying levels of complexity: a book, a house, and a town.

Let us consider the book. The first relationship that we notice, through the handling of the book, is the one between *inside* and *outside*. Something is *in* the book and something is *out* of the book, which means that the space of the book that is presented to us is separate and

---

20   Henri Lefebvre, *La production de l'espace*. Paris: Éditions Anthropos, 1974.

21   I provided a more precise analysis of this example in Marcello Vitali-Rosati, 'Perceptibilité du virtuel et virtualisation de la perception', in *La transition du perçu à l'ère des communications*, Pessac: Presses universitaires de Bordeaux, 2013, pp. 191-206, http://www.lcdpu.fr/livre/?GCOI=27000100180410. The same structure is described by Pierre Lévy as a 'virtualisation of space': Pierre Lévy, *Qu'est-ce que le virtuel?*, Paris: Éd. la Découverte, 1995.

individuated. It is important to stress that we *produce* this relationship by handling the book. The relationship between inside and outside is not given. The fact that there is an inside and an outside at all depends on the action of picking up the book; while still sitting on the shelf, the book is involved in the production of space in a completely different way. By looking at the shelf we can, create another kind of relationship altogether – the one between on and off the shelf – a relationship that exists on a different plane from the one that handles the book itself. There is an inside and an outside to the book only because we do something: that particular action is the context that allows for the production of an inside and an outside. When one handles the book in order to read it, its inside and outside are thus produced. Back on the shelf, the inside and outside are not pertinent anymore: in their place a relationship between 'on' and 'off' appears. At the same time, however, there is also something in the book itself that structures its space, a particular organization that is already there before our action; before we handle it or look at it. This means that the production of space is always circular: it emerges from a dialogue between what is already there, and our way of traversing and inhabiting that which is given.

The publisher has employed numerous strategies to make it possible for a reader to identify the inner and outer space of a book, and these strategies are the result of many years of publishing tradition. The book has a cover, which is harder than the leaves of the book, there is a text block on the back, there is a particular way of binding the leaves with the cover, et cetera. We are accustomed to understanding and interpreting this structure, and as a consequence we are able to produce other relationships: for instance, between before and after. A book has a direction – a beginning and an end – and we are immediately able to produce this direction by holding the book in a certain way (the correct way) before setting out to read it. Because of our left-to-right way of writing and reading, we will hold the book closed so that its spine is to our left and the side that opens is to our right. In this way we are able to examine the front cover of the book, which we understand as its beginning, in an upright position. We know that the text will start from here and that the whole book will be organized from this direction. There is a linear relationship between the objects in the book: the letters, words, and pages appear one after another. As we read the book – another action – we produce this linear relationship. It is a two dimensional relationship: objects cannot be one *on* the other, just one *after* the other. I stress again that we *produce* these relationships by reading the text: if we look at a book without reading it, we can produce some relationships between the sheets of paper that sit atop one another. If we give the book to someone who cannot read, they will organize the space of the book in a complete different way. The linear relationship between the words has a meaning only if somebody can actualize it by his reading action. When we read, a complex dialogue starts between something that is given – the text as it has been written – and something that is created in the very moment of the action of reading. We can skip pages, skip words, read from right to left – for example in order to correct the orthography – or look for a particular passage on a particular page. In all these cases the organization of space of the book will be taking on a different shape.

The notion of 'text' itself suggests that the organization of space is the result of a production process. The Latin verb from which the word text comes is *texere* whose first meaning is *to weave.* A text is a fabric, that is, a set of relationships between a multitude of threads that are produced in the act of weaving. Writing a text signifies to weave relationships between objects. Also when we read a text, we are weaving it: to read means looking at a fabric in order to create paths by following threads. This idea anticipates some of the discussion that is addressed in the second chapter of this book. The web, it can be said, can be productively understood as a form of text: it too is a fabric, something that is weaved.[22] The choice of metaphor is important: like a spider web, the web is a set of relationships built between objects and like a spider web this set of relationships is produced when traversing it.

Now let us consider the example of a house. That the relationships between objects in a specific space are created at the very moment that the space is inhabited is quite clear with a house: a house becomes a home depending on how it is inhabited. If we consider our own home against some other house belonging to a stranger, it is obvious that the relationship between inside and outside in the two cases is different, even if the two buildings are identical. So, in the case of a house, it seems, we have the same complex dialogue between something that is there, that is given, and our actions. On one hand we have walls and windows, pipes, wires, on the other hand we have the inhabiting the building and how one inhabits it; both produce relationships between objects and thus produce a space. A wall can define the relationship between two rooms, but this relationship will be different according to how one inhabits them, for example if one uses them as bedroom or as living room.

With a house, as with a book, the first relationship that can be identified is the one between inside and outside. Some architectural elements – like the threshold – allow us to move from one side to the other. It is interesting to note that the paratextual elements of a book (the title, the name of the author, etc.) can be interpreted *as* thresholds; Genette, in fact, proposes this metaphor in his book about paratexts.[23] Once we are in the house, many relationships characterize the inner space: relationships of visibility, of audibility, of crossability. The space of a house is this set of relationships. From every position there is something we can see and something we cannot see, something we can hear and something we cannot hear. Our notions of privacy and intimacy are founded on how visibility and audibility are structured. Our way of inhabiting our home and traversing it produces and changes these structures. The fact that something is visible is thus not only the result of a given organization of space, but also of how we inhabit it. On the one hand, this is because we can actually move things and change the organization. On the other hand, it is because we produce habits and values that structure the space: we can or we cannot enter somebody else's room, we can or we cannot sleep in the living-room, we can or we cannot play music in the kitchen or watch the television when eating. The set of relationships that constitute the space of a house implies at the same time a set of values: the meaning of privacy and intimacy, as mentioned earlier, but also the power

---

22   Hypertext is another way of weaving, another way of producing relationships between objects. This has been analyzed, for example by Christian Vandendorpe, *Du papyrus à l'hypertexte: essai sur les mutations du texte et de la lecture*, Paris: La Découverte, 1999, http://vandendorpe.org/papyrus/PapyrusenLigne.pdf.
23   Genette, *Seuils*.

relationships between the inhabitants of the house and gender relationships. This deep link between space and values is explored by Beatriz Preciado in the book *Pornotopia*.[24] She demonstrates that certain architectural changes in the conception of a house give rise to radical shifts in values: from the family centered way of living as it is personified in the middle-class house to the playboy's philosophy of the penthouse.

The town offers both the clearest and the most complex illustration of how space can be understood as a set of relationships between objects. In a town, as with a book or a house, one can identify a clear relationship between inside and outside, though in the case of a town there is also a complicated membrane system to consider: the threshold of the town such as its suburbs, its periphery. And there is also the complex and multidimensional 'text' of the town. A map will give an idea of this text: we see a complex system of threads which links different spots. Streets, squares, bridges, but also public transport lines, boundaries between different neighborhoods. The objects in the town have relationships of distance, of visibility, of accessibility, depending on the architectural structures in place: the streets, how these streets are built, how traffic is regulated, how intense it is, how the public transport system works, how much it is frequented, and during which hours.

It is easy enough to see that the space of a town is made up of relationships between objects and that these relationships are the result of the inter-operation of architectural elements and the practices of the inhabitants, what they actually do and what their habits are. At the same time, there is also a town plan that works to create relationships between objects and between places. This plan might be pre-established by some institutional power, such as the munici-pality. In a sense, this plan precedes the practices and the actions of the inhabitants. It is also *made* by the practices and the actions of the inhabitants, however, by their ways of moving in the town, their ways of organizing their days, and their activities. And if we take the analysis a step further, it becomes clear that one cannot draw a sharp line between a pre-established plan and the actual space of the town, conditioned by the actions and the habits of its inhab-itants. Here again, the separation between a given space and a dynamically produced one is completely theoretical: there is not on one hand the space of the town given by an architectural plan made by a central power, and on the other hand a particular way to inhabit this given space. The town is built in an organic way which is driven by people's uses and practices.

Space and Writing

If space is a set of relationships, what, in concrete terms, are these relationships? How are they made? Of what are they made? One of the problems with talking about space in these terms is that one could be tricked into thinking that the relationships of which it is constituted are immaterial or abstract or in no way concrete. In other words, there is a risk of thinking of space as simply an idea, as something that can be manipulated according to how it is conceptualized. I have said that a space is not given. However, this should not be taken to mean that a space is completely flexible or that it can be reshaped as we want. In other words,

---

24   Beatriz Preciado, *Pornotopia: An Essay on Playboy's Architecture and Biopolitics*, New York: Zone Books, 2014.

the question to which we must find an answer is: does space have objective qualities or is it completely subjective? The notions of objectivity and subjectivity of the space can be linked to the notions of materiality and immateriality: one could say that a space is objective if it is material and that it is subjective if it is immaterial.

Boris Beaude insists that space is not material precisely because it is produced in the very moment we inhabit it.[25] But this idea is ambiguous: we might *think* that we can produce space just as we like, without being confronted with any resistance. Space risks to be a completely subjective notion. What needs to be stressed, however, is that a space *is* materially constituted insofar as it is something that imposes limitations on what we do. Space is the context of our actions and to a certain extent it shapes and determines them: it is thus objective. The notion of materiality is difficult to grasp, of course. Often, something is defined as immaterial in order to say that it is irrelevant, simply because then it is unformed and unclear. And, not surprisingly, the concept of immateriality is often used to define digital space. Digital space is said to be 'immaterial' in the sense that it's supposedly not structured, but 'liquid', disorganized, anarchic. Using the rhetoric of immateriality is also a way for web companies to hide the actual political and social implications of some of their products or practices. For example, 'cloud computing' is a metaphor that suggests that our data are immaterial, that they are nowhere, that they are light, and thus that they do not cost anything, that they are not on a particular hard-disk of a specific computer in a specific place, owned by a specific company. The 'cloud' metaphor as such is a way of forgetting all the economical, geopolitical, and social implications of a particular material infrastructure.

One of the aims here is to show that we cannot understand the specificity of the digital if we keep thinking about it as something immaterial. We can start by giving a definition of materiality as something that offers some kind of resistance to our activities. Something is material insofar as it prevents us from doing one thing and forces us to do something else. Working from this first definition will allow us to reconsider the three examples discussed earlier – the book, the house, and the town – in order to understand the extent to which they are material, and whether it is possible to reconcile the seemingly opposing facts that they are given material spaces *and* spaces that we produce by inhabiting them. My demonstration will be based on a particular interpretation of the notion of 'writing', which is understood here as a very broad notion. Writing is the action of producing a permanent trace, a trace which stays inscribed somewhere after the end of the writing action. In this sense, the act of writing some letters on a piece of paper is a sort of writing, but so too is the action of drawing a line in a field in order to delimitate a border between two proper-ties, or the action of opening up a path in a forest by cutting some trees. Writing means leaving a trace. It is important to emphasize that these traces are something material, they are inscribed somewhere – on a piece of paper, on a field, on a territory. They are never imaginary. Each space, I will argue, is made of material, inscribed traces. In this sense my interpretation continues on Maurizio Ferraris' theory of documentality.[26] In this theory

---

25   Boris Beaude, *Internet, changer l'espace, changer la société: les logiques contemporaines de synchorisation*, FYP éditions, 2012, http://www.beaude.net/icecs/.

26   Maurizio Ferraris, *Âme et iPad*, Parcours Numériques, Montréal: PUM, 2014, http://www.

Maurizio Ferraris criticizes Searl's theory of collective intentionality.[27] According to Searl, social rules are based on some shared principle which are a part of what he calls 'collective intentionality'. This means that a group of people consider an interpret an object in a particular way because they share a collective way of seeing the world. However, as Maurizio Ferraris observes,[28] this theory has a problem, because how concretely does this collective intentionality express itself? Therefore Ferraris states that every social rule has to be written in order to exist. The point that I want to underline here follows from that, namely that there is no immaterial way of structuring a space: each space must be structured by something which is inscribed somewhere, a permanent material trace.

An example can clarify this idea and the meaning of writing. The space of a book is made up of writing in its more common meaning: permanent traces of ink on some papers and the relationships between the objects – letters, words, pages, and so on – within this space are also written. We have already identified two of those: inside/outside and before/after. Others can be added, such as relationships of visibility (more/less visible, if we consider for instance the relationship between a title and a paragraph), or textual relationships (text which refers to other text like a footnote or an internal link). Each of these relationships is something written. The inside/outside relationship is determined primarily by the paratextual elements: the text that we find on the cover allows us to understand that what we find after the cover is *in* the book, and what comes before is *out* of the book; the chapters' titles tell us that some text is in the chapter while other text is not, and the author's name points to what portion of a text is a part of the author's discourse, and what portion is not. The before/after relationship is made by the written characters that appear one after another, and by the direction of the writing. The relationships of visibility – how visible a particular object is compared to the others – are also written and depend on the shape of the writing (bigger or bolder fonts, with or without italics, etc.). And finally, the textual links are written: with use of a footnote or a sentence such as: 'as I said in the first chapter'.

Despite the seemingly inscribed elements of these relationships, however, they are not given: they appear only as somebody actually reads the book. The space is thus made through a set of operations which are not only written. Somebody has to read the book in order to actualize these relationship. The structure of the space of the book is thus the result of a double process: the writing process and the reading process. But what kind of action is 'reading'? The act of reading a book is not the isolated action of one individual. The individual is inscribed in a broader set of relations. When I read a book, I create relationships between objects, but not in a way that is entirely free; I cannot do what I want. Reading demands respect for some rules, and these rules determine what I can and cannot do. My hypothesis is that the rules that allow us to read must be themselves written in some way. This means that the complex process of producing and interpreting a space can be understood as a form of writing, and that reading is itself a form of writing. So, what does this mean?

parcoursnumeriques-pum.ca/ameetipad.

27   John R. Searle, *The Construction of Social Reality*, New York: Free Press, 1997.

28   Ferraris, *Âme et iPad*.

The fact that, when we take a book, we are able to produce relationships that are the basis of the book's space must depend on something. We could, with Searle, affirm that it depends on a collective intentionality.[29] As I said, according to Searl's theory, a group of people consider an object in a particular way, and they interpret it in a particular way. This theory could be summarized with a formula: 'X counts as Y in context C'. In the case of a book, the formula would be applied along these lines: 'this block of sheets counts as a book in this society at this moment' (say, in Montreal in 2017). That this block of sheets counts as a book means that there is a collective interpretation of what a book is. Moreover, this interpretation brings with it a set of rules that allows us to understand how to handle the book and how to read it. However, I think Maurizio Ferraris[30] is right when he observes that this theory has a problem: it is based on the possibility of certain immaterial rules which can express this collective intentionality. But how would that work, concretely? In order to be able to collectively consider a block of sheets as a book we must have some documents that explain to us what is a book and how to read it. These documents are written in the broad sense that I have defined: they are inscribed somewhere. They could also be inscribed only in the neurons of our brain, for instance, but this is still a form of inscription. This implies that every social rule has to be written in order to exist. Ferraris therefore proposes a change to the Searle formula. Instead of 'X counts as Y in context C', it should be: 'Object=recorded act': or, a book is a book because we have documents that explain to us what a book is. This idea is exactly what Ferraris calls 'documentality'. We can summarize by saying that a book is a book because it is written in a certain way and because there are other written documents – outside the book – that allow us to understand how to read and how to interpret the book. The relationships that make the book's space are thus writing/reading relationships, but the reading part is itself made by writing.

In the case of a house, it is obvious that there is a written structure that makes a house a house. The architecture of the house is a form of writing. A wall is a written trace that creates a relationship between one room and another. It is a material inscription. A window is a written trace that shapes numerous relationships of visibility – i.e., where I can see, what I can see, where I can be seen. The clearest expression of the structure of a house's space is the architectural plan on which the relationships between different objects in the house are written: the rooms, the furniture, and other physical features. Beyond the written structure, however, these relationships have a meaning only because we interpret them in a particular way. A bedroom is a bedroom because there is a bed – and this is something written, a materially inscribed trace, namely the fact that the bed is actually there – but also because we sleep in it. The relationships of visibility, to name an example, certainly depend on the fact that there is a wall separating the bedroom from the living room, for instance, but also on the fact that we consider the bedroom as an intimate space. We would not go into the bedroom of a person we do not know very well. In other words, the space of the house is created by something that is written *and* by our way of reading it.

But, as said, our way of reading and interpreting this writing depends on documents that are themselves written. There is a material document that attests to who owns the house, to give an example. This document allows us to interpret the relationship between inside and

---

29   Searle, *The Construction of Social Reality.*
30   Ferraris, *Âme et iPad.*

outside, but also it allows us to understand the whole structure of the space. The first thing that we must know when we go in a house is the identity of the owner. This frames, among other things, the relationships of visibility: can I enter in the bedroom or is it a private space to which I do not have access? There are other material documents that establish how a house is occupied, how its rooms are used; they establish the designated purposes of a living room, a kitchen, a bathroom, and so on. All these 'cultural' elements which define our collective way of interpreting the world are material, inscribed traces which can be found in certain documents. These documents are books, or movies, or other written cultural objects that are the basis of our education and that allow us to interpret in a common social way the written relationship of a house's space. Once again: the space of a house is a set of writing/reading relationships, but the reading part is itself a kind of writing.

The set of relationships that make the space of a town is also written. There is a plan for the town that establishes the shape and structure of the streets, the location of the buildings; there is a plan for public transportation, a plan of every building which is recorded and archived somewhere, and many other documents. The space of the town mixes in a deep way the writing and the reading part. The boundaries of a town can exist only because there is a document that establishes them; without this document – which is the result of complex political negotiations and agreements – it is impossible to interpret the relationship between inside and outside: where does the town begin? What is part of it and what is not? Thus the space of a town is the result of the superposition of many written layers: plans, documents, streets, buildings. Each of these layers is made of material traces inscribed somewhere – on a piece of paper, on a territory, on a street. We inhabit the space of a town without being completely aware of this complex structure, but it is only because this structure exists that we are able to understand the very meaning of a town. Without this complex writing/reading system, without this set of documents, it would be impossible to understand, for instance, what downtown and uptown means, what is a neighborhood and even what a street is, what a building is, what the difference between a shop and a house is. In the case of a town Ferraris' critique to Searle seems consistent: how can a collective intentionality which is not written be the explanation of the boundaries of a town? Actually nobody could ever define these boundaries, they would be an abstract concept if a recording of them wasn't kept somewhere in order to guarantee their existence.

An objection to this thesis could be that there are societies in which the rules which allow us to interpret the world are carried on an oral tradition. In oral societies there are not written documents. But still these rules are actually written in the broad sense of the term: they must be inscribed in the brains of the members of the society: this is why they are material. Human memory is another form of inscription: it is a trace written and inscribed in a living organism, but it is still a trace. If we kill all the members of an oral society we lose these rules and there will be no ways of understanding and inhabiting the space.

The fact that a space is written is the reason why it has to be considered as something material: documents present us with a form of resistance because we cannot modify them without some form of action – and this action can be very difficult. If a document establishes the limits of a town and somebody has a house that is outside these limits, they cannot say that their house is in town. It is possible to extend the limits of a town, but it demands a complex process. In the same way that one cannot read a book without applying a set of reading principles, one cannot inhabit a house without respecting the function of every room. Or, to be more precise: one can change these principles, but it implies a visible action of alternative use. One can sleep in the kitchen and cook in the bedroom, but these would be declarative acts that call into question the meaning of specific spaces. This idea of alternative/critical use (which can be expressed with the French word 'détournement') is something that we'll return to in the final chapter of this book.

We can summarize by saying that the space is the set of relationships between objects and that these relationships are always something written. This is why a space is always something material: it is written and this writing opposes to us some sort of resistance.

Space and Politics

The examples we have looked at so far suggest that each particular structure of a space is somehow related to a set of values. A space is not only a layout of objects; it also implies a particular interpretation of the world. In other words, writing and reading a space means producing a particular point of view of the world as well as a particular way of inhabiting it. This means that *the process of writing/reading a space is strongly political*. With regard to this point, the interpretation of space-production proposed here is different from Lefebvre's idea. According to Lefebvre there is a precise hierarchy of the elements which contribute to the production of the space: some of these elements are more material than others. Typically, according to Lefebvre, all the elements related to the cultural way of interpreting a space are less important than the elements related to the infrastructural structure of the space: a highway structures a space in a stronger way than the cultural perception of what an highway is. Enrico Agostini-Marchese underlines that this hierarchy is problematic because the cultural representations of space are deeply entangled with the other elements.[31] We could add that, according to the documentality theory of Ferraris, all these elements are written, and that for this reason they can be seen as positioned on the same level. This allows us to understand why our cultural interpretation of a space – our way of 'reading' it – is also a way of writing it. Enrico Agostini-Marchese in this context refers to the notion of *nomos* as developed by Carl Schmitt:[32]

> This untranslatable term reveals a fertile polysemy for our reflection: originally designating the place reserved for grazing, nomos gradually came to mean "sharing", "division involving an idea of order" and finally "use", "custom having the force of law" as well as the law itself. In this perspective, a spatial rooting generates practices which then become normative.[33]

---

31   Enrico Agostini-Marchese, 'Les structures spatiales de l'éditorialisation: Terre et mer de Carl Schmitt et l'espace numérique', *Sens Public*, 10 March 2017, http://sens-public.org/article1238.html?lang=fr.

32   Carl Schmitt, *Land and Sea*, Washington, DC: Plutarch Press, 1997.

33   Agostini-Marchese, 'Les structures spatiales de l'éditorialisation'. Translation by the author.

Initially, the nomos is a permanent inscribed trace: a line which creates the boundary between two fields. The cultural signification is later derived from this first material act of 'writing' the territory.

We will illustrate this idea by taking up the analysis developed by Beatriz Preciado in her *Porno-topia*.[34] One of the main ideas developed in the book is that *Playboy* magazine introduced a new conception of domestic space, and in doing so deeply changed social and political values. In particular, *Playboy* developed the idea of the penthouse, a domestic space that marked a significant departure from the space of the traditional middle-class house. The most important innovation of the penthouse was its blurring of the relationship between in and out, visible and invisible, vertical and horizontal. This was in sharp contrast to the middle-class house, whose architecture produces a clear separation between the interior and the exterior. The middle-class house is often far from the center of the town and far from public space. It is detached, isolated. The inside is characterized in contrast to the outside: the inside is the space of the heterosexual couple, the space where one rests, the space of the woman, the space of privacy. The outside is the space of society, of work, of men, of the public sphere.

The inner space is also structured in itself: the rooms are clearly separated from one another and each has its own function. Some rooms are more private – the bedroom is the most private, the one that is most 'inside' – while others are more open, such as the living room. Some rooms are meant to be visible, some invisible. This structure produces a specific conception of society: the common occidental middle-class vision of the world typical of the 1950s. The penthouse re-organized these relationships between in and out, visible and invisible and private and public. The playboy apartment is situated downtown: in the middle of public space and in the middle of working space. The spatial structures are also different; there is no clear separation between in and out, between private and public, between the private and the public sphere. This implies a radical change in the behaviors and most of all in the values of the inhabitants.

In order to better illustrate this idea I will turn to a scene from Stanley Kubrick's *Eyes Wide Shut* (1999), a film that is particularly useful as a way of explaining the deep link between space and values. The film is based on a clear division between two components of space: a red one and a blue one. The photography of the movie shows this separation, which seems to structure every frame. The two colors are initially related to the inside (the red) and the outside (the blue). Indeed, from outset it is clear that inside is red; it is warm, calm and protected. The inside is the space of the family, in this case the middle-class family of Dr. Hartford and his wife. The outside, in contrast, is blue, it's cold and hostile. In the opening scenes, inside the Hartfords' apartment, everything is red but the windows. The colors seem to be related only to the physical – or architectural – structure of the space. But soon enough it becomes clear that the two colors are also functionally connected with the characters: Mrs. Hartford is red and her husband is blue. Red is the color of the woman, blue the color of the man. Starting from this connection we can surmise that the structure of the space described in *Eyes Wide Shut* has a deep relation with a particular vision of the world and of the society. The man is an outside creature – which means that he is the one who works, the one who deals with

34   Preciado, *Pornotopia*.

society, the one who is exposed to its dangers. He is also the one who stands, which is another spatial characteristic. The woman is an inside creature: she stays at home, she raises the children, she guarantees the intimacy of the space, and thus of the couple's fidelity and love. And, naturally, she lies down. This is a clear description of the American middle-class family's values, values which are expressed through spatial organization. Even the gender dynamics are defined by the structure of the space.

Eyes Wide Shut is a film about values and about the structure of the space that produces them. In the scene of the first crisis, when the Hartfords smoke a joint together, the binary structure of the space is brought into question. The scene begins with a split frame: one half is red and is occupied by Mrs. Hartford, who lays down on the bed; the other half is blue and is occupied by Dr. Hartford, who stands in front of a door. On one side is the woman: a symbol of intimacy, of fidelity and the love of the couple. She is passive and fragile. On the other side is the man, actively standing in front of a blue door, ready to go out. But soon there is an inversion: Dr. Hartford goes to the bed and lies down, while his wife stands up in front of the window. The man becomes red and the woman becomes blue: this is the beginning of the crisis. It is the moment when Mrs. Hartford starts saying that she is not faithful 'by nature' and it is the beginning of the complex narrative sequence of the movie. The spatial inversion implies an inversion of values.

This is exactly what the notion of nomos as used by Enrico Agostini-Marchese means: a spatial structure – the line delimiting two field – implies a particular way of understanding and carries values which become rules. Moving from this observation, we can identify some important structures of a given space in order to analyze their relationship with the production of values. The analysis I propose is neither exhaustive nor the only one possible, but it should help to give an idea of the political implications of space, which will be analyzed in the last chapter of this book. I will list three main structures. These structures define how the relationships which characterize a particular space are made and why they have political implications:

1. *Delimitation.* The first thing to know about a space is what is inside and what outside. The inside and the outside are the first relationships that make a space comprehensible. But the notions of inside and outside clearly have political and ethical implications. The inside is related to membership, to belonging, to friendship. The outside is related to the other, to the enemy, to what is hostile. Understanding the delimitation of a space is necessary in order to understand its rules. Only by knowing the limits of a space we can understand how it works and what it means. And, on the other hand, in order for a rule to be effective it is crucial to know the limits of the space to which it refers. Delimitation is the characteristic of a space that allows us to make a political distinction between the private and public spheres. This distinction is one of the foundations of democratic societies. The public and the private spheres are regulated by different rules: this means that the sources of authority are not the same in these two spheres. The delimitation then is the structure that makes it possible to have a plurality of sources of authority. As we have seen, the very possibility of an authority depends on the identification of its spatial limits: the authority of a state, the authority of a *pater familias*, the authority of a doctor, and so on. This means that if we change the delimitation of a space, if we move its limits, we also change the rules of the space, the principles

of its authority, and thus its values. The example of playboy architecture, as analyzed by Preciado, is particularly clear: the delimitation of the family space and the social space is sharp. This delimitation is the basis of a specific idea of the family, related to specific ideas about gender. Playboy proposes a different way of delimiting living space. The separation between the inside and the outside of the apartment is not related anymore to a separation of the public and the private spheres. The playboy's apartment is a space where work and rest are merged, where there is no longer a clear distinction between what is private and what is public. The open space allows the kitchen and the living room and the bedroom to be brought together. And in this way, the activities that are linked with each space are commingled: one can move from the living room to the bed without any rupture. The play-mate – the 'girl next door' – can enter the playboy apartment like a normal neighbor – maybe to ask for some milk – but there is no separation between the hall and the bedroom, and there are no limits that impose a clear threshold between the public sphere and intimacy.

The sexual behavior of the playboy is based on a parallel radical shift of values. Preciado argues that this change in spatial organization results in a modification of gender relations. The absence of a clear separation between inside and outside blurs the distinction between women and men, and thus marks the end of a sexuality based on middle-class family values. In the traditional family's space, the delimitation of inside and outside functions to classify people: it is, first of all, a classification of family members and then a way of determining the relationship between people who belong to the family and people who do not belong to it. It is always possible within this context of delimitation to say whether someone is *inside* the family or *outside* of it. Each person is or is not allowed to enter into the intimacy of the family space. The penthouse's space, in contrast, does not invite this distinction to be made. The limits of the playboy's space are not given: they move according to what the playboy is doing; his space is extended as far as he goes. There is no longer a space that is reserved for intimacy and another for public activities; there is no longer a separation between work and pleasure; there is no longer a separation of genders.

2. Position. The structure of position describes the relationship between objects after the limits of a space have been identified. In a town, for instance – which is a delimited space – there is an area that is considered to be the center and an area that lies on the borders of this center. The notions of *center* and *border* define the position of an object by comparing it with other objects within a given space. The relationship between *up* and *down* offers another example of position: like the position of a floor or the position of one person compared to another. Center and borders, up and down, left and right, above and below, in front or behind, north or south – these are all attributes of position. Position is intimately related to hierarchy and in a more general way to all relationships of power.

Let us take another example. In most Christian towns – especially those with medieval origins – the cathedral is in the center of the city. The position of the cathedral can be used to determine if one is downtown: Notre Dame in Paris, St Peter's in Rome, Westminster in London. This association marks a clear signal of the power of the Church. Its power is located in the center so that it can exercise its control throughout the entire space. The fact that the cathedral is in the middle of the town is a political issue because it implies a particular organization of political power. Pisa is an exception to this organization: in the middle of the city stands the Palazzo dei Cavalieri, which was previously the Palazzo degli Anziani, the town hall of the medieval maritime republic, i.e. the headquarters of the temporal power. The cathedral and all the other religious buildings are in the Piazza dei Miracoli, which is on the border of the city, next to the defensive walls. These positions signal a different organization of political power: the temporal power in this case is more important than the religious one. The organization of political power can also be expressed through horizontal or vertical position. The case of *Eyes Wide Shut* is a good example: the vertical position in the film signals a dominant attitude: the man who stands is raised above the woman who lies down. In the same way, the position of a teacher in a classroom shapes her or his power relation with the students: every student has to look up at the teacher when he or she is standing, or the teacher is located higher than the students on a platform.

3. Distance. Distance is another structure of the relationship between two objects. The primary characteristic of distance is that it is an attribute of quantity. An object is more or less distant from another object. One could think that for this reason distance is an objective attribute that has nothing to do with values or interpretations. But, as demonstrated earlier, this is not the case. A distance is a particular way of writing and reading a space. The distance between two towns is the result of the constructions of roads, transportations and other elements of infrastructure, as well as of many other social and political factors, such as the importance of the towns, their representation in people's imagination, the traffic, the cost of the roads, the existence of borders, the belonging of the two towns to the same state, the same culture, the same region, and so on. The same analysis is valid for other examples of distance: the physical and social distance between two persons – the very idea of which has been deeply modified by the social networks and that will be considered in the following chapters – or the distance between two pages of a book. Distance is a way of measuring the intensity of a relationship and thus of evaluating its importance. In other words, distance is a key factor in the construction of a taxonomy. A space is a set of relationships and this set is organized and classified. Relationships are not all on the same level and distance is used to give to each relationship a particular position within the whole. The classification produced by distance has a clear impact on our values. Indeed, through this classification a society finds its priorities. The visibility, accessibility, and, finally, importance of each object depend on its distance from where we are. We care more or less about somebody or something depending on their distance from us. We know more or less about something depending on how far away it is.

These structures demonstrate that an attentive analysis of space allows us to understand the social and political values that are behind it. *Understanding a space means understanding a political organization.*

Space and Authority

Now let us come back to the question of authority. I said earlier that every manifestation of authority is based on a particular structure of space and that a given space always comes with a particular set of political values. This means that understanding a space allows us to understand the manifestations of authority that are associated with it, and at the same time to have a critical awareness of that authority. But what exactly is a critical awareness of authority?

An authority, after all, is something we trust without argument, which means that we do not have to understand the reasons why the authority is right. We trust an authority because it is an authority. At the same time, it is crucial to realize that every authority that we trust is regional in the sense that it is valid only within the particular structure of space in which it is situated.

Understanding the structure of a space allows us, first of all, to identify its limits and thus to make relative its validity. What is valid and reliable in one particular organization of space is not necessarily valid and reliable in another. This means that an authority is a principle related to a specific political organization and thus to a specific set of values. These values, as we showed, emerge from a particular structure of space. Understanding the structure of a space allows us to understand that there is no absolute authority because every space has its limits, otherwise it would not be a space.

It is true that an authority imposes itself without having to justify itself, but it is also true that it imposes itself always as something regional, something particular, something that has limits. Authority is a spatial issue and the very possibility of our understanding the particular political frame in which an authority is valid rests on our understanding of the space in which it is found. This is the only way to distinguish between authority and political violence, because an authority without limits, an authority that would be valid everywhere and in every space, is not an authority (as the term is being used here) but an absolute and tyrannical power that imposes itself regardless of any particular political frame, affirming its values as if they were universal.

In other words, the aim should not be to determine whether (or why) an authority is reliable but rather to figure out *where* it is reliable. In fact, it is not possible to decide if or why an authority is reliable because this would mean that we are able to identify some political or ethical principle that is valid in a universal way, that is, independent of a particular space. Political values are inseparable from the organization of the space, however. A critical awareness does not give us the ability to understand the rationality of an authority. There is no rational argument for trusting an authority because of the very definition of the authority; we can only understand its perimeter. But the understanding of the perimeter of a specific authority offers the basis of the possibility of freedom: it allows to possess the knowledge that what we trust in one context – in one space – is not valid elsewhere, in another space. Thus no authority is absolute; it is always relative to some ethical and/or political frame that is specific to a particular space.

We now come to the main question of this book: Is the internet bringing about an end to authority? One could say that the network deconstructs all spatial structures, that it is a non-space, an unorganized set of heterogeneous objects and that for this reason it is impossible to identify authority within it. This argument can be used optimistically or pessimistically: the disappearance of authority offers the possibility of emancipation; or it results in a general disorientation, a loss of principles and values. I hope to demonstrate in the following pages that both these arguments are based on a false premise, that the network is in fact a very well organized space – or, to be more precise, a set of differently organized spaces. Understanding these spaces and the values that lay behind them is crucial to an understanding of what authority is in the digital age.

3. THE STRUCTURE OF THE DIGITAL

What is the Digital?

The word 'digital' is more and more present in the public discourse. A quick look at Google Ngram Viewer is enough to see that the use of the term has been increasing steadily for twenty years, especially in some bigrams like 'digital communication', 'digital culture', or 'digital space'. Even the nominalization 'the digital' has entered into use. Digital is not only an adjective that characterizes certain tools or technologies; it has become an object, even 'an object of analysis'.[35] But what do we mean exactly by the term 'digital'? What is 'the digital'?

It is impossible to reduce the term to its first meaning: digital is a particular way of representing information, in opposition to analog. *Analog* is a form of representation that has the same shape as the original – and thus is continuous with its reality – while *digital* representation is achieved by translating the continuity of the real into discrete numbers through a sampling process in which a continuous signal is cut into a set of discrete 'samples'. In this basic sense, a CD is digital, and a vinyl record is analog. Moving from this initial definition, we have begun to use the term *digital* to describe all kinds of tools and computer-based technologies. The *digital*, in other words, has begun to have more far-reaching cultural significance[36]: it is used to express a range of cultural changes. Indeed, the term digital is not strictly related to particular technologies anymore. As Milad Doueihi has shown, the digital is modifying every aspect of our lives and in this sense its cultural impact is comparable to the impact of religion: becoming digital and adhering to a digital culture is a shift that is not unlike the change a religion brings forth. Thus the technologies that are present in our lives have a tremendous influence on our way of inhabiting and interpreting the world.

The term *digital* is therefore used to express not simply a technology but rather *a set of changes that characterize contemporary societies in comparison to what they were twenty or thirty years ago*. The increasing use of this adjective and its emergence as a commonly used noun, suggest that we are struggling with something new. The prevalence of the word can be interpreted as a sign of unease caused by changes that have impacted the way certain institutions function. In this sense, the digital has no precise meaning: anything can be described as digital if it is somehow new and if the fact of its being new can lead to a disruption of institutionalized behavior.

The fact that the word digital begun to be used more and more from the 1990s suggests that a crucial shift occurred with the birth of the web. In terms of technology, the web has had a visible impact on our practices and has triggered significant changes in our way of life. But is it quite right to think that the digital has produced a revolution? Can we accurately interpret the changes brought about by the birth of the web as a rupture in our culture? Numerous scholars have analyzed the idea of revolution and found that in it, there are always aspects of both continuity

---

35   Patrik Svensson, 'Envisioning the Digital Humanities', *digital humanities quarterly* 6, no. 1 (2012), http://www.digitalhumanities.org/dhq/vol/6/1/000112/000112.html.

36   Milad Doueihi, *Digital Cultures*. Cambridge, Mass.: Harvard University Press, 2011.

and discontinuity.[37] The digital is a cultural phenomenon and as culture is always continuous, it is necessary to understand the digital too as part of a continuity of tradition and not as a revolution. In other words, the digital does not represent a genuine rupture that breaks the line of history. This may seem to contradict what I said earlier, where I talked about an important change in the structures of authority: if there has been no revolution, if the change we refer to has occurred in continuity with a culture's history, then why would we perceive such a shift regarding authority? I have compared the current shift – that is, the shift to the digital – to the change produced by the Protestant Reformation in the 16th century. But if these shifts in actuality do not engender a rupture in our history, then what exactly do they signify? A shift is discrete, it is a passage from one particular point to another, clearly separated and recognizable. A shift in this way indicates a break with continuity. But how can it then be possible to sheathe such a break precisely with the idea of a cultural continuity?

The fact is that, even if it is true that our history and culture are continuous, not characterized by ruptures, it is also true that our institutions change in discrete ways. So while our practices, customs, and habits – like our technologies and our way of inhabiting the world – change in continuous ways over time, not like an evolution or a progression, but just as a slow and continuous modification, our institutions, for their part, are there to normalize our practices, our customs, and our habits. In order to do this, institutions must measure the status of our practices, customs, and habits at specific times, as though they were taking pictures of society at specific moments and offering snapshots of our behaviors. Of course, when a given moment has passed, practices continue to change until they are quite different from the first picture that institutions have taken. Therefore a gap will emerge between the reality of practices, customs, and habits, and the way institutions describe and normalize them. And this gap brings forth a change in institutions: a discrete change, a shift. This is why, at the very moment when institutions have to change because of an ever-widening gap between its norms and the reality of practice, we speak about revolution or rupture

Let us consider the example of what we could call, with Eisenstein,[38] the printing revolution. Should the invention of printing be considered as a rupture in our history? Certainly, the technical invention itself can be understood as part of a continuity. There is never a radical shift in technical innovations; they are always integrated in a continuous process. But we can identify an institutional shift – or, to be more precise, a series of institutional shifts. It is interesting to note that the institutional frame for the printed edition was established and normalized during the 18th century, at least two hundred and fifty years after Guttenberg's invention of movable types, which took place in 1455. At the beginning of the 18th century, England promulgated the Statute of Anne (1710), the first copyright law. As Rose has shown,[39] this paved the way for the institutionalization of the print-based economic model. Printing became a normalized and regulated practice: the role of authors, their

---

37   For example, Milad Doueihi, *Pour un humanisme numérique*, Paris: Seuil, 2011 and Luciano Floridi, *The 4th Revolution: How the Infosphere Is Reshaping Human Reality*, New York, Oxford: Oxford University Press, 2014.

38   Elizabeth L. Eisenstein, *The Printing Press as an Agent of Change*, Cambridge: Cambridge University Press, 1980.

39   Mark Rose, *Authors and Owners: The Invention of Copyright*, Cambridge, Mass.: Harvard University Press, 1993.

responsibilities and their rights, the function and the tasks of the publisher, and the relationships between different publishing houses were regulated by the law. States adapted themselves to these new practices by changing their laws and their principles; and these changes were necessarily made in a discrete way.

Practices have progressively changed since the 18th century. The role and the function of the author and the social perception of what an author is have all changed, as have the technical devices used for reading, the readership, including the number of people able to read, and the economic and social conditions. Practices are so different from what they once were when institutions first normalized them, that a sense of unease has arisen: institutional norms are no longer able to regulate or to understand actual practices. The word digital is a symptom of this unease. We are aware of the fact that something different from the institutional field is going on, but we do not know exactly what it is or how it is structured. 'Digital' is the word we use to express this blurry gap between institutional discourse and actual practices. More specifically, in the case of the edition, the expression 'digital edition' is used to signify a set of continuous changes that separate current practice from the 18th century's habits. This need to find a name and to identify the specificity of current practices is a sign that institutions need to change to adapt themselves to the reality of new practices. Thus, we are in an institutionalization phase.

One defining characteristic of the digital is that it signifies the necessity of upgrading a large number of institutions in many different realms. These include personal identity management, teaching, research, art, and communication. The digital is not – or at least not only and not primarily – about computers and technologies: it is a term that is often used synonymously with 'current'. We could even say that it is on the same level as 'modern' or 'contemporary'. After the modern age and the contemporary age, we are living in the digital age. Technology is certainly an important aspect of digital culture, but not all aspects of culture are determined by technology. Rather, there is a circle of determination: technology is determined and shaped by cultural tendencies and culture is in turn conditioned by technology.

The change we see in authority should be understood in this context. As discussed, authority is based on the structure of a given space. Digital is the word we use to express a set of cultural changes, as well as the gap between current practices and institutional discourse. Among the most noticeable cultural changes associated with the digital is a transformation in how space is understood: this is why authority has changed as well. Again, it should be emphasized that this change is not a revolution: our habits and our practices have changed progressively over centuries and now the authority model on which our institutions are based is no longer adapted to the reality.

Cyberspace

If we understand the word digital as suggested in the previous pages, it is evident that digital space is really nothing more than actual space. The space in which we live is digital space – exactly as our culture is a digital culture. Again, in this respect when we talk about digital space, we do so in the same way that we talk about modern space or contemporary space.[40] Digital space in this sense is not something separate, something that is elsewhere, a parallel space. Digital space is the space of our digital societies, a space that has changed because of a complex set of cultural and technological shifts. Moreover it is important to note that, as in the case of 'modern space' or 'contemporary space', the singular 'digital space' signifies a plurality of different spaces with different structures and values. This space is not completely new compared to older forms of space. Rather, it should be understood in continuity with other spatial structures that have characterized societies during their long histories.

The most common interpretation of digital space, does not recognize this element of continuity. In the public discourse, at least, digital space is mostly understood as a parallel space, separated from 'real' space and often interpreted as imaginary. In this chapter I will show that this interpretation is useless and even damaging, and that it does nothing to help us understand the changes implied by the digital.

The idea of a separate and parallel space first took hold in the 1980s, mainly in the realm of science fiction. The term 'cyberspace' was popularized by William Gibson in his 1984 novel *Neuromancer.*[41] The prefix 'cyber' is taken from the word 'cybernetics', which comes from the Greek word *kybernetes,* meaning 'pilot' or 'governor' – in particular, the governor or the captain of a boat. In the term *cybernetics*, the prefix helps to express the idea of a self-regulating system. Cybernetics, as defined by Norbert Wiener,[42] is 'the scientific study of control and communication in the animal and the machine'. Obviously, in the scientific notion of cybernetics, there is no reference to fiction or to the imagination. In science fiction, however, authors like Gibson link the idea of a self-regulating system to an artificial world: cyberspace is a parallel world that is regulated by machines, i.e. artificial. The fact that this parallel world is isolated and self-standing can suggest the idea that it is therefore also fictitious. But this equation is actually false. In science fiction a system's ability to regulate itself is related to the fact that it is isolated. A system that is self-standing and regulated by a machine is associated with its separation from reality and it thus being unreal. The fake syllogism that science fiction seems to suggests here is this: if a system is self-regulated, it is thus artificial; and if it is artificial it is necessarily unreal. This obviously fallacious argument has been fruitful for science fiction stories but quite useless for cybernetics and for scientific efforts to understand how digital space is made and to identify its characteristics.

It is important to underline this deep link between cyberspace and science fiction. The link is far from accidental, and science fiction's vision of digital space has deeply influenced the way we commonly understand that space. As I have already shown,[43] cyberspace has been

---

40   This idea can be related to the notion of 'post-digital' as it is used in arts. In 2000 Kim Cascone underlined that the digital revolution is over: we now live in a post-digital era. See Kim Cascone, 'The Aesthetics of Failure: "Post-Digital" Tendencies in Contemporary Computer Music', *Computer Music Journal* 24:4 (2000): 12-18.
41   William Gibson, *Neuromancer*, New York: Ace Books, 1984.
42   Norbert Wiener, *Cybernetics: Or Control and Communication in the Animal and the Machine*, New York: John Wiley & Sons, 1946.
43   Marcello Vitali-Rosati, *S'orienter dans le virtuel*, Paris: Hermann, 2012.

embraced by literature as a figurative construct that functions as a *mise en abyme*. Literature – and in particular the novel – offers a parallel world. The literary world, the world of the story, is an imaginary world that pretends to produce a parallel space: the space of *diegesis*. In the literary experience, the reader always has to deal with a continuous shift from extradiegetic space – their space as a reader – to diegetic space – the space produced by the text, the space where characters live. Blurring the boundary between these two spaces is one of the most common proceedings of literature. The goal is to give reality to the literary experience: the reader should not be able to know with certainty whether they are living something real or unreal because they don't know which space they're actually in while reading. This kind of blurring, even if we do not actually believe it, gives reality to literature. The *mise en abyme* is one of the most common ways for blurring the boundaries between diegetic and extradiegetic space because it creates additional layers that lead the reader to become lost.

So, in the space of a novel we create a parallel space in which exists another parallel space, which contains yet another parallel space... and so on. The same structure can be found in cinema. The 1999 Cronenberg film *eXistenZ* is a good example where this trick is played out in a telling extreme: it tells the story of an immersive video game that takes place in a parallel digital space. When playing, the participants are completely invested in the artificial, digital space created by the game. In the game's world, the players can play another immersive game in which they are again invited to play a game... and so on. At the end it is impossible to know the layer on which the players find themselves. Are they still in the game? Or in the game inside the game? Or in the game inside the game inside the game? Or have they returned to reality? Of course, 'reality' in this instance is also a fiction because it is a movie reality. But this becomes more and more blurred because of how the different spaces are tangled. And, paradoxically, this has the effect of making the film seem more real. Even if this proceeding is nothing but a trick and even if the reader and the spectator do not actually believe in it, it seems that this trick has often been interpreted in the first degree; the structure was used frequently in the literature and cinema of the 80s and 90s and in that way influenced our idea of cyberspace. Cyberspace was associated with a parallel and fictitious space by linking it to diegetic space. But the growth of internet connections during the 90s, along with the birth of the web, gave rise to something new: the word 'cyberspace' began to be used in reference to the space of the internet, or, to be more accurate, the space of the web.

In this sense, cyberspace can be associated with the notion of the infosphere as defined by Floridi:

> Minimally, infosphere denotes the whole informational environment constituted by all informational entities, their properties, interactions, processes and mutual relations. It is an environment comparable to, but different from, cyberspace, which is only one of its sub-regions, as it were since the infosphere also includes off-line and analogous spaces of information. Maximally, infosphere is a concept that can also be used as synonymous with reality, once we interpret the latter informationally. In this case the suggestion is that what is real is informational and what is informational is real.[44]

---

44   Floridi, *The 4th Revolution*, p. 41.

Floridi crucially points out here that cyberspace is only a *part* of the infosphere. In fact, not all information is online, not all information is in digital space. But this evidence is not really pertinent if we use the term digital in a wider sense, that is, as it was defined above. Digital is not only what is online; it is the very structure of our reality in the time of digital tools. In this sense, I propose to interpret the expression 'digital space' as a synonym of infosphere and to abandon the term 'cyberspace', which is too strongly associated with science fiction. Digital space is not a parallel space, nor is it a part of our space: it is the *only* real space that we can inhabit. Or to be more precise, all the spaces we can inhabit are digital.

If 'digital' is the adjective that most effectively characterizes our space, what exactly does this adjective say about that space? What are the specific characteristics of the space in which we live today? How is it different from other kinds of spaces, for example, modern space?

A Space of Writing

In the first chapter I described space as a set of relationships and suggested that these relationships are made of writing. I also suggested that there is a deep link between writing and reading; indeed, one could say that there is actually no form of reading that does not imply a form of writing. In other words, a space is a set of writings and readings that establish a set of relationships between objects. In this way, a given space defines an organization; it structures the framework in which we live.

The hypothesis that I propose here is that *digital space is the organization of the totality of our reality thanks to writing*. This is another way of explaining the notion of infosphere: the overlapping between information and reality. In order to demonstrate this hypothesis, let us start from an analysis of the web. Again, we should not simply identify the web with the digital because the digital is a generic concept that can be used to characterize our entire reality. But the web is undoubtedly one of the main causes of the emergence of the digital as an important category. One could say that our world and our culture have become digital in part because of the web. The web is thus one of the most important phenomena of the digital world. Understanding the web can help us to understand the characteristics of digital culture.

The first thing to say about the web is that it is made of writing: everything on the web is written, even the pictures, even the videos. Everything is code. And this code has the function of creating a peculiar layout of relationships between objects. In this sense, the web is mainly an architectural space. And this space is, in turn, characterized by a mix of writing and reading, which is the property of every space. In fact, the relationships structuring the web exist only as a function of the actions concretizing them and these actions are writing and reading.

Furthermore, the space of the web is concrete; it is neither immaterial nor fictitious. Its objects – whether data, information, documents, or identities – entertain material relationships with one another. There is a precise and distinctive distance between two objects on the web, exactly as there is in non-digital space. Between my Facebook profile and another, there is a measurable distance – the quantity of friends separating us, or the rules of confidentiality as I have defined them. Between a given web page and another there is a distance determined by the degree of connection between them – a direct link, a search engine, a co-affiliation with a list.[45]

In this space actions are carried out. Following Paul Mathias,[46] the web should be considered fundamentally as writing. The actions of the web are written actions: to act on the web means to write. Indeed, most digital practices constitute writing in its most direct sense: we write a blog post, we write our Facebook 'status', we write a comment on an article, we chat with a friend through the chat of some social network, we write the words for what we are looking for on a search engine, we write the URL in the address bar. But these are not the only kinds of writing associated with the web. Other practices are less easily identifiable as writing: clicking and reading, for example. Clicking is one of the most common actions on the web, whether it be simply the action of clicking a link, moving to another page, or hitting the 'I like' option on Facebook. Careful scrutiny reveals that clicks in fact produce writing; traces of code are written on databases – in the case of 'I like', for instance, or in the caches of certain servers – in the case of the click on a link. In this sense, even a reading path creates writing. To read a page and then another in effect means to create a link between these two pages, a link that is registered, under a series of characters, on a computer. Internet providers are obligated to register the overall reading path of its clients and so each click creates a material link between pages and objects. The action of the click thus contributes to the structure of the space.[47]

Let us consider a more complete example: the simple and frequent experience of looking for a book on Amazon. One arrives at the main page – or to the page of a particular book if one has used a generic search engine like Google. Then one clicks on some links: maybe the link of the publisher or the author, or maybe something else on the Amazon search engine. In this way, one arrives at some other book's page. In doing so, the user is creating a link between these two books' pages. The clicks are recorded in the Amazon database and so a relationship is created between two – or more – objects. The two books are linked and this information will in turn structure the digital space in which they are placed. Other users will be able to see this relationship. For example, the Amazon algorithm may recommend the second book to users who buy the first one. By clicking on a link, a user reduces the distance between two things, just as if he were taking two books from a library and putting them on the same shelf.

In other words, the idea that the web is a space is not simply a metaphor. The web is an actual space, a concrete and material one, because it structures relationships between objects. We live in this space and we build and structure it with our actions, especially the action of

---

45   Marcello Vitali-Rosati, 'Digital Paratext: Editorialization and the Very Death of the Author', in Nadine Desrochers and Daniel Apollon (eds) *Examining Paratextual Theory and Its Applications in Digital Culture*, IGI Global, 2014, http://www.igi-global.com/book/examining-paratextual-theory-its-applications/97342.

46   Paul Mathias, 'De la dychtologie', in Eric Guichard (ed.) *Regards croisés sur l'internet*, Lyon: ENSSIB, 2011.

47   We can understand many other practices related to mobile devices like cellphones and tablets in the same way. A gesture like swiping is another form of clicking; when one swipes, one is actually adding an information in a database. Swiping in that way is another form of writing.

writing. The web is a part of the space we inhabit, but it influences our whole space. In the first chapter I showed how a space is always made of writing. But in the case of the web, this characteristic is even more pronounced and undeniable. Digital space is characterized by writing. Everything in it is a kind of writing: its relationships, its actions, and its perceptions are all forms of writing.

A Space of Actions

Let us analyze more precisely how the web is a space of action. This idea questions the very notion of a parallel space. As said earlier, the web is not a parallel space but a part of our actual space. In fact we act *in* the web – I say 'in' and not 'on' because we are talking about a real space, one in which we are actually involved.

First of all, I propose a minimalistic definition of action: I call 'action' everything that one can do. In a more formal way, we could say that an action is everything that can be expressed with a verb. An action can thus be active or passive; playing is an action, like perceiving, loving, or dying. Action is a movement, a process, something that implies a motion. In this sense, writing is an action with the property of leaving a trace of movement.

The web is an environment in which many actions of our daily life take place. Let us consider some simple daily activities that we act out on the web. I follow the news, which can be text on a newspaper site or videos on a television site or on a generic platform like YouTube. I then look for something on Wikipedia, perhaps a topic linked to the news I have read; and from there I click on other Wikipedia pages. Next, I conduct a search on Amazon for a book on the same topic and I decide to buy it in a Kindle edition. After that, Google Calendar reminds me that I have a meeting with a colleague. I am late, so I send – still on the web – an email to my colleague to propose that we meet via Hangout. He writes back to tell me that it is fine. I now have an hour to spare, so I decide to check my bank account and pay my rent, which I do electronically on my bank's website. Waiting for the call from my colleague, I remember that I wanted to write a review of the restaurant where I ate the day before. I do this on the TripAdvisor website. Finally, I have the conversation with my colleague, with whom I'm working on a paper. We are using a web-based text-editor in order to work simultaneously on the same document. We finish our work and then send the paper to a journal for publication.

Clearly, a huge portion of our daily activities now takes place on the web. I could continue to list my web-related activities indefinitely. But let us examine this particular list of actions one by one and try to understand their meaning and what they consist of.

The first kind of activity that I cited involves some form of reading. Indeed, reading is probably the most common thing we do on the web. According to my minimalistic definition of action, reading is without doubt an action: it implies a movement and a process. The example of reading the news is instructive on this point. As many scholars have pointed out,[48] reading

---

48   See, for example Espen J. Aarseth, *Cybertext: Perspectives on Ergodic Literature*, Baltimore: Johns
       Hopkins University Press, 1997; J. Yellowlees Douglas, *The End of Books or Books without End?:*

with digital support, especially on the web, is a particularly active action. One could say, of course, that reading has never been passive, in the case of reading on paper (as Eco stresses in his *Lector in fabula*),[49] because a reader creates the meaning of what they're reading and that *act* of creation is clearly a form of action. But in the case of digital reading, the element of action is even more evident.[50] In order to read the news, I first search for it – probably by typing the name of the newspaper I want to read on Google, or by typing the URL directly in the address bar. I then decide to click from one page to another, producing a particular path that did not exist before my action of reading. The interesting point about this path is that it is written. All my clicks are recorded and written somewhere, which means that by clicking my way on to a page and then on to another I have created a material link between these two pages. This link can then be used by an algorithm to recommend one of these two pages to users who are on the other one. My reading is thus a form of writing. By reading a newspaper and then clicking on a YouTube video or a Wikipedia page, I have written a path linking these pages. This written path functions as a road connecting different points and different objects. Conceivably, in this example, I would purchase a book on Amazon after these readings. The fact of buying is clearly an action; I actually move some money and I take part in determining the movement of an object, the book. In the next chapter we will examine how the difference between the book itself, as an object, and the description of the object that one finds on the Amazon site, is less clear and is probably disappearing.

The actions I refer to above are also written, of course: they are characters in a database – where one can find my name, my address, the list of the books that I have consulted and bought, the comments that I have left, and so on. This writing is the very structure of the Amazon book shop. And like a non-digital bookshop (I do not want to say 'actual' or 'material' because Amazon *is* an actual and material bookshop), Amazon organizes the books in its database spatially – as on shelves. What are the criteria on which this system of organization is based? There are certain classical taxonomic criteria – like the genre, the topic, the author – but there are other criteria as well that are based on the behavior of the company's customers. These behaviors are actions that structure the very architectural space of the Amazon bookshop: clicking on a book is much the same as moving a book from one shelf to another in a non-digital bookshop. This means that in the digital space we encounter the same structure of writing/reading that we saw in the previous chapter. On one hand, there exists in this digital space something that determines our actions and structures them: like the wall in a house, something that is already written imposes on us a particular behavior; it directs us in certain ways. On the other hand, by reading this space we actually rewrite it, producing new structures.

Reading Interactive Narratives, Ann Arbor, Wantage: University of Michigan Press, 1999; Bertrand Gervais, 'Naviguer entre le texte et l'écran: penser la lecture à l'ère de l'hypertextualité', 2002, ; George P. Landow, *Hypertext: The Convergence of Contemporary Critical Theory and Technology*, Baltimore: Johns Hopkins University Press, 1992; Sarah Sloane, *Digital Fictions: Storytelling in a Material World*, Stamford, Conn.: Ablex Pub., 2000; Vandendorpe, *Du papyrus à l'hypertexte*.

49   Umberto Eco, *Lector in fabula*, Paris: Librairie générale française, 1985.

50   Aarseth (*Cybertext*) states that digital text cannot be compared to printed text because the form of interactivity is completely different: in the case of digital text reader's actions change the very text that s/he will read; in the case of printed text the text is the same and only the interpretation changes.

The fact that I use an online agenda – like Google Calendar – means that my daily organization is also written digitally and so comes to occupy the same space as other forms of digital writing. My click on a Wikipedia page becomes a set of characters in a database, just like the memo for my meeting. It is another example of how something written structures our actions: the memo is already there – even if I am the one who wrote it – and it shapes my actions. These actions exist in a sort of continuity, whether they take place prevalently in digital or in non-digital space. I am late and so I write an email that reorganizes my schedule. The communication with my colleague is again a form of writing – both the email and the Hangout are recorded as a list of characters on a server. Even videos constitute writing, in the most basic sense: a video is encoded as a series of characters' strings which are recorded on a physical device – a hard-disk. The YouTube algorithm which allows subtitles to be automatically added to videos is another proof of the deep relationship between video and text: the sound of a video can be automatically transformed into text, with a relatively accurate result, and of course also analyzed as such. The discussion that I have with my colleague by email is another action that consists of writing and that becomes part of the structure of the space where it takes place. For example, Google will use what I write to my colleague in order to send me targeted advertising. Google's semantic algorithm[51] reads my email and discovers that I am talking about a paper that I should present during a conference in Ottawa on May 23rd. Google's algorithm might suggest a hotel in Ottawa or a train for the journey. In this way, my writing has structured the digital space and influenced the behavior of an algorithm – and in return the algorithm can influence my further behaviors.

Paying the rent is also an action that is made of writing. By connecting to my bank's website and paying my rent I change the number that stands for the amount of money in my account and I change the number in my landlord's account as well. Obviously I can do this only by respecting some pre-established rules: I must subtract an amount from my account to add something to my landlord's account, and I must give something to the bank. The rules are themselves written; they were built into the code of the algorithm that guides the transaction.

Finally, the TripAdvisor review is obviously an action made of writing. Indeed, it is writing in the most common sense of the word. What is interesting to note about this writing, is that, once again, it molds the structure of the space: in contributing to the classification of the restaurant, I move it up or down a list. In doing this I am not only changing the structure of the digital space – where the restaurant is located in the space of TripAdvisor – but, most importantly, I am moving it spatially in a more general sense because I am modifying its visibility and changing the kind of customers it will have.

As the above observations should make clear, we act on the web and our actions are always a sort of writing. Even the reading that we do on the web is a kind of writing. Writing is the very material of which digital space is made.

---

51   For a general description of Google activities see Randall Stross, *Planet Google: One Company's Audacious Plan to Organize Everything We Know*, London: Simon and Schuster, 2009.

Reality and Virtuality

The description of typical daily activities that take place in digital space should demonstrate beyond doubt that the idea of a parallel, imaginary space is not an effective or accurate way to describe what was once called cyberspace. Digital space is the space we normally inhabit; it is where we live our daily lives: digital space is our space. Nevertheless, I think it is important to briefly analyze another concept that has often been used to characterize digital space: the notion of virtuality.

First of all, it's worth noting that the word *virtual*, which was prominent in the discourse of the digital until about ten years ago, is steadily disappearing. A quick look at Ngram Viewer will demonstrate this point. Until 1979, the term 'virtual' was a technical notion, used in physics and philosophy in order to express certain specific theories. In the 80s, the word started to be used in relation to new technologies, especially in the bigram 'virtual reality'. The idea behind this expression is clearly that we can artificially create a parallel space which is *like* reality but which is not *the* reality; it is a fictive world.

Scholars no longer describe digital space as 'virtual'. The critique of this notion of a fictive space has been at the center of many books.[52] All these critics underline that our digital practices are mostly related to our everyday life and thus they are not fictive at all. Although it is true that we recently witnessed the rise of many new projects dealing with virtual reality – Oculus Rift by Facebook being the most known – these projects are clearly meant for entertainment and do not challenge anymore the boundaries between reality and fiction. The dream of virtual reality as a confusion between real and virtual was among the most enticing of the promises made by technological industries in the 80s. Today the commercial discourse seems to bet more on the notion of *augmented* reality, which has progressively substituted the idea of virtual reality. And augmented reality, as the term suggests, refers not to a parallel space but to a coexistence; it occupies the same space with different layers of information, which may or may not be digital.

Curiously, the application of the word *virtual* as it came to be associated with what we now think of as digital is quite different from the original philosophical meaning of the term. Passing through several physical theories – in particular, optics – the earlier meaning of the concept evolved and it eventually became a synonym, or almost a synonym, of fictive. However, as I have already shown in previous books,[53] going back to the philosophical meaning of the term can help us better understand some of the characteristics of digital culture.

What strikes me as particularly pertinent is the fact that 'virtual' means something that is in progress. Something is virtual when it is going on. Aristotle states that 'virtuality (dynamis) means a source of movement or change'.[54] Virtuality is the force that produces the movement and the

---

52   See for example Lévy, *Qu'est-ce que le virtuel?*; Stéphane Vial, *L'être et l'écran comment le numérique change la perception*, Paris: Presses universitaires de France, 2013; Vitali-Rosati, *S'orienter dans le virtuel*.

53   Vitali-Rosati, *S'orienter dans le virtuel*; Marcello Vitali-Rosati, *Corps et virtuel: itinéraires à partir de Merleau-Ponty*, Paris: L'Harmattan, 2009.

54   Aristotle, *Metaph.* Δ 10.

virtual is what is moved. In this sense, virtual is everything that is in motion, i.e. everything that is going on in the very instant it is going on. This is another way of saying that everything real is virtual, if we understand reality as the totality of what is going on. In others words, in a dynamic conception of reality everything is virtual.

Now, it is obvious that a dynamic conception of reality is not exclusive to digital culture, but we could say that it is one of its defining characteristics. 'Real time', for example, is a common phrase that expresses the sense that everything is in motion and that we cannot stop this movement. We could even say that every conception of the world is characterized by a more or less dynamic way of describing reality. There are two extremes that can be applied here: on the one hand, there is the idea that movement does not exist; on the other, there is the idea that essences do not exist because everything is always in movement. The former idea is traditionally attributed to Parmenides and the Eleatic school: movement is an illusion because in order to understand the world we must look at the essence of things, which means that we must look at what a thing is beyond its movement: what it is and how it remains in time. Reality, in this view, is an actualization of movement. The other extreme is an anti-essentialist idea of the world, an example of which is Heraclitus' famous *panta rhei*: everything flows. According to this point of view, reality is always virtual and we cannot speak of an actualization because actualizations are only abstractions. It seems clear to me that digital culture is closer to this second conception; this is why digital space can be called virtual.

Liquid or Structured

A dynamic conception of reality introduces an obvious problem: it can imply the impossibility of grasping things and understanding the world. Everything flows and thus it is impossible to know anything because it all slips out of our hands constantly. If digital space is virtual, it is also liquid; this could mean that it has no structure, or at least it does not have a stable structure that we can analyze and understand. If this argument is true, then it is also true that authority is at its end. One cannot speak about authority if the space in which this authority should act is an unstructured space. The argument can be formulated thus, following on the previous chapter: every authority is based on a particular structure of space; digital space has no structure; therefore, digital space has no authority.

But this is far from true. The fact that digital culture is characterized by a dynamic idea of reality does not necessarily imply that digital space is unstructured. Digital space is dynamic in part because, as we saw earlier, it is made by writing and reading. Although digital space, as every other space, can be said to be in movement, this does not mean that it does not have a clear structure. The structure of digital space has certain characteristics that are different from other kinds of spaces that we're familiar with. This may explain why we sometimes have the feeling that it lacks structure: it is new to us and therefore not easily interpretable. Behind this apparent lack of structure, however, there exists an architectural space, a very well organized one that is not so difficult to analyze. Because digital space is a written space, we need only to read its writing to understand its structure.

In the first chapter we identified three fundamental kinds of relationships that structure every space: delimitation, position, and distance. Digital space is an architectural space in the sense that it is a set of relationships that define the delimitation, the position, and the distance between a set of objects. In other words, for every object, digital space structures a relationship of delimitation, of position, and of distance in relation to another object or other objects.

With this in mind, we can reconsider the idea that digital space blurs the boundaries between objects or that it implies a deterritorialization.[55] It is, I think, more accurate to say that digital space reconfigures boundaries and restructures territories in different ways. Let us start with the first kind of relationship that structures space: delimitation. A particularity of digital space is that the same object can be a part of more than one set without having to be multiplied. In contrast, a non-digital object can only be in one place at a time. In the case of a book, for example, this means that one must choose which shelf to place it on in a library. Let us take a printed copy of Aristotle's *Physics*. This book could be placed in the philosophy section or in the physics section. But a library must choose: the same book cannot be in two different places unless the library buys a second copy. This is not true for the digital version: it can be placed in any number of generic categories without the need of additional copies. I can tag the electronic version of the *Physics* with the label 'philosophy' and with the label 'physics' and the same object will be a part of two distinct categories – two different spaces. This does not mean that the two sets – philosophy and physics – are not structured. In fact, there is both a structure and a logic: all the books that relate to physics go to the physics section and all the books that relate to philosophy go to the philosophy section. But the spatial logic is different. With the printed book, the classification principles are more complex: all the books that relate to philosophy and more so than to other sections go to the philosophy section. The logic of the library classification system had to be adapted to the specific characteristics of a printed object: such an object cannot be at the same time in two different spaces and we cannot in practice respect the fact that a book can belong to two different sections – unless we have another copy of the object itself. As this example shows, digital organization of space is in some ways more logical than that of printed material. It is also more structured. Digital space actually allows respect for the logic of classification. But because we are used to dealing with the constraints of the printed model, we tend to think that digital space is not structured. Libraries have tried to resolve the problems coming from the limitation in classification of printed objects by creating complex indexes and files; digital space is in a way only simplifying a spatial organization that has existed for a very long time – at least since the Library of Alexandria. This illustrates the main difference between digital and non-digital space as it pertains to the element of delimitation: delimitation is often exclusive in non-digital space and often inclusive in digital space[56] – a characteristic that will be discussed more specifically in the next chapter.

When we look at digital objects, we realize that they are largely organized on the basis of delimitation: every object belongs to a set – or, more likely, to many sets. This is evidence of the sturdy structure of digital space. The fact that this kind of delimitation is not exclusive, however, generates an impression of openness. As we will see, although this openness is in

---

55   Michel Serres, *Atlas*, Paris: Julliard, 1994.
56   On this topic see Doueihi, *Digital Cultures*; Vandendorpe, *Du papyrus à l'hypertexte*.

fact a logical characteristic of digital space, it is not always true that digital space is open. An object may belong to different sets, but there are forces that influence its classification. For instance, if Amazon decides that Aristotle's *Physics* should not be considered a physics book, the company's decision has more impact on the delimitation of the category 'physics' than a decision that I might make when categorizing the book on my private blog.

Once the limits of a given space have been identified and once we know what is inside and what is outside of it, we can analyze the position of an object in relation to the space. In the first chapter we discussed how the *position* is the set of relationships that one object has with other objects in the same space. For non-digital space, we used the example of the town and we analyzed the structures of center and borders, and of up and down, as attributes of position. The characteristics of the position of an object in digital space are determined by the specificity of delimitation: because delimitation in digital space is not exclusive, an object can occupy several different positions at the same time. This could be interpreted again as a lack of structure in digital space: that is, one could say that objects have no real position because they can be in many positions at the same time. This could be used as an argument to prove that digital space is liquid, that it has no actual structure and, by extension, that it has no authority. But once again, if we study it more attentively, we'll realize that there is no absence of structure. An object can occupy several positions at once because it belongs to several different spatial frames. However, these frames are very well structured or even rigid – sometimes more rigid than the frames that we find in non-digital space.

Let us consider again the example of a book. This time let us imagine that we are looking for Luciano Floridi's *The 4th Revolution*. In a brick-and-mortar bookshop, this book would occupy only one position. It might be in the philosophy section, where it would be ordered by the author's name. We would therefore find the book under F in the philosophy section. This position reflects a set of relationships that the book has with all the other objects in the bookshop: the other books, the shelves, the walls, and so on. The book will be placed 'after' one book and 'before' another. It will be up or down in a bookcase and the bookcase on which it sits will be central or not in relationship to the other bookcases in the bookshop. The fact that the delimitation of the space is exclusive implies that the book has only one position. The book is 'in' the philosophy section, which means that it is necessarily 'out' of the communication section – or any other section, for that matter. The book is 'in' one bookcase and thus 'out' of the others.

In digital space the situation is different. First of all, let us be clear that we are talking about the same book: the printed edition and not – or not necessarily – the digital one. The printed edition of *The 4th Revolution* exists in digital space: I can buy it on Amazon or on another site; I can talk about it on my blog or post a comment about it or review it in an online journal. Digital space, as I said earlier, is not only the space of computers; it is our space in general, the space in which we live. Even a bookshop of printed books is part of this space; the proof is that its economic model is changing in response to developments in digital space. Let us imagine that we are looking for a book on Amazon. The first difference between Amazon and the bricks and mortar bookshop is that my Amazon is not the same Amazon that another customer encounters. For instance, when I open the Amazon website *The 4th Revolution* may appear on the home page as a recommendation. The book is showcased for me but not for another customer. Its position and visibility are different. At the same time, the position it occupies in *my* Amazon is structured and well defined. The position is far from *liquid*: indeed, the fact that the book is showcased prominently on the page leads my behavior to some extent by alerting me to its existence and so triggering me to wonder whether I want to buy it. As we will see, position is very much linked to values: the showcased book becomes more important than others. Of course, the book occupies multiple positions: it is simultaneously showcased for me and *not* showcased for another customer; it is in the philosophy section but also in the communication section, and so on. This multiplicity actually depends on a complex – and unique – description of the book. *The 4th Revolution* on Amazon is a set of data that is continually analyzed with the help of an algorithm. All the data are properties of the book, which can be used in order to set multiple types of relationships between this and other objects. If, in the old-style bookshop, the data about *The 4th Revolution* are relatively poor (the author, the title, the publishing house, the discipline), on Amazon we have these same data as well as data about other customers who liked the book or who bought it, data about the sales statistics, data about the keywords describing the book, which are related to other keywords describing other books a specific customer has bought, and so on. All this information can be used or not according to the specific details of each use case. Which means that, depending on the information used, the book will have different relationships with other objects and thus different positions. So, on the one hand, we have a general set of information, which is rich and complex; on the other hand, we have many particular positions that are produced on the basis of this set of information, whereby each position only expresses a part of the whole set of information.

To repeat, this structure of digital space is not completely new; we cannot consider it a revolution. If we look again at the example of the book in a bookshop, we can easily see that the same book could have many positions if there were many copies of it. In this sense, the printing revolution moved things in the direction of multiplying the positions of an object. And, more generally, the industrial revolution enabled the emancipation of objects from uniqueness and allowed such kind of multiple positioning.[57] The specific characteristic of the digital is that it develops on existing structures and not that it creates them from nothing.

The third aspect that structures a space is distance, which in this context is a measure of how far or how close an object is from another object in a given space. During the 90s, after the dramatic increase of internet connections in houses and the development of the web, many scholars advanced the hypothesis that in the digital space there is no such thing as distance: this is the notion of deterritorialization,[58] which holds that there is no territory online because everything is immediately accessible and so there is no longer any place for distance. Twenty years later, this interpretation no longer seems an efficient way to describe what happens in digital space. The distance, in fact, between objects is perhaps the most important aspect of

---

57   See Benjamin's theory of reproducibility and its adaptation to digital objects by Maignien: Walter
      Benjamin and Michael William Jennings, Brigid Doherty, Thomas Y. Levin, and E.F.N. Jephcott (eds).
      The Work of Art in the Age of its Technological Reproducibility, and Other Writings on Media, Cambridge,
      Mass.: Belknap Press of Harvard University Press, 2008; Yannick Maignien, 'L'oeuvre d'art à l'époque
      de sa reproduction numérisée', 2 January 1996, http://archivesic.ccsd.cnrs.fr/sic_00000302.
58   Serres, *Atlas*; Lévy, *Qu'est-ce que le virtuel?*.

digital space and this distance is always measurable and it is necessary to do so in order to be able to act online. The key difference between position and distance is that position is about knowing where an object is located – for example, up or down, or central or in the periphery – while distance is about knowing *how* up or down this object is, how central or removed it is. Thus distance is about quantity. We are often unconsciously aware of distance in digital space: proof of this is the importance that we give to the ranking of pages on the Google research list. PageRank creates a map by attributing a score to each page: this score is the distance between the page and the pertinent keywords. The shorter the distance, the higher up the page is on the list. When a user consults the list to find the most pertinent results, they are completely aware of the fact that there are pages that are either closer or further away. A user may even feel that moving further away from the first page and the top result demands more effort than staying close. 94% of users do not scroll past the first page of Google results.[59] The top position is clicked on more than the others. This should be recognized as evidence of distance in digital space: closer things are more accessible than things that are far away. Which means that distance is crucial in digital space.

Every object in digital space can be defined by the distance between itself and other objects, even if this distance changes according to shifting configurations. In the case of the search engine result list, a different search engine could (and probably would) assign the same page a different distance, thus changing the attributes of its distance. But this could also happen in non-digital space. As Lévy points out,[60] building a railway between two cities creates two alternative distances between them, one in which the cities are separated by a train journey and the other by for example a walk. This number of distances is multiplied as new technologies – such as train, plane, car, or telephone – create new configurations of space.

Clearly, the importance and the calculability of distance are not new; they do not apply only to digital space. Still, the importance of the element of calculability is particularly evident in digital space. We could always determine the distance between two towns, by examining a map and calculating how many kilometers separated them. But with digital objects these numbers must always be a matter of consideration. The computer depends on them and it cannot work without them. The necessity of distance in digital space can be easily illustrated: there is a distance between two Facebook profiles – which is calculated using the Facebook algorithm and allows the platform to decide which content to show on the wall of each user; between two books on Amazon – which are different for each user and which allow the platform to maximize the sales; or between two webpages – whether on a search engine or according to the links separating them: the distance between two platforms or two profiles on two different platforms or some variation of these. In the next section we will discuss the relationship between these spatial attributes and a vision of the world. Space, we will see, determines values.

The Values of Digital Space

---

59   Gresham Harkless, 'Importance of Showing up on the First Page of Google – The Unique Side of Entrepreneurship', *The Unique Side of Entrepreneurship*, 18 July 2012, http://progreshion.ceopress. com/2012/07/18/importance-of-showing-up-on-the-first-page-of-google/.
60   Lévy, *Qu'est-ce que le virtuel?*.

A spatial structure carries values, as discussed in the opening chapter of this book. Thus digital space, with its special characteristics, implies a specific framework of values. When considering this idea, it is important to avoid two opposing and fallacious arguments regarding the relationship between digital space and values. The first one has to do with the assumption that digital technologies are tools that are completely neutral with respect to values. This is a naive view that is based on the idea that a tool can allow us to do something faster and more easily and yet not change the action itself or any aspect of the accompanying behavior. The implication is that a tool does not carry any inherent values; everything depends on how we use it. This opinion is misguided in that it isolates the tool from the context in which it emerges, as though one could speak about it without knowing anything about its context. But this is clearly false: we can think about and understand a tool only by situating it in the social context in which it is used. We have to understand why the tool has been made, for what purposes, from what materials, under what constraints; otherwise, we will not be able to understand how it can be used. If we situate the tool in a more complex context, we realize that it is not neutral at all, that its uses are to a certain extent predetermined.

This leads us to an opposite, yet equally fallacious, argument, the one that basically states that the digital automatically determines certain behaviors, and we could therefore express moral judgments about it. Following this logic, one could say that digital space is good or bad, that it implies more or less freedom, that it implies more or less humanity, etc. One could say, for example, that digital space leads us to read more – or less – and that this is bad for our society – or good. Or one could say that digital space increases violent behavior – or decreases it – and that, again, this is bad – or good. It is important to underline that these statements, which are of course very common in the public discourse, exist in both positive and negative form, which shows that there is no strong logical argument for one or the other. This is why we often have two factions: those who support and those who oppose new technologies. But both these factions are wrong because their arguments rest on the idea that one can separate moral values from the context in which they appear. On the one hand we would have moral values and on the other we would have technologies. We could try to judge whether a given technology is good or bad, as though it were possible to measure it with a meter. But the problem with this approach is that moral values are shaped by cultural context, and the context of our society is a digital one. Hence, what we need to understand is not whether digital technologies are good or bad, but rather what kinds of values they produce. This is what the idea of *nomos* expresses, as we've already seen earlier. Structuring space implies a particular vision of the world and a particular negotiation on rules and values. In *The Nomos of the Earth*, Carl Schmitt shows that the original meaning of 'nomos' was an act of land-appropriation.[61] The social rules and norms are a consequence of this land-appropriation, which means each space carries its own values.

Digital space is not neutral but, at the same time, it does not automatically imply a particular set of behaviors. Rather, it contributes to the formation of a particular framework of values, as every space does. What we try to understand here is the specific framework of values that is produced by the particular structure of digital space. Beyond this, we want to know how this space shapes

61   Carl Schmitt and G.L. Ulmen, *The Nomos of the Earth in the International Law of the Jus Publicum Europaeum*, New York: Telos Press, 2006, pp. 67-79.

our way of interpreting the world, as well as our moral and political values. Finally, we want to identify how this particular framework implies a specific conception of authority. Once again, digital space is neither more nor less authoritative; it only produces a very particular notion of what authority is. Understanding the structure of the digital and the values it produces is crucial to developing a critical approach to these issues. If we know the rules, we can criticize them; if we identify the structures, we can – if we want – try to find different ones. At the very least, we will understand why we have certain values instead of others.

Let us return for a moment to the three aspects of digital space we have just analyzed. I do not think that they provide the only way to describe the structure of a space, but they are useful to understand its principles and its way of working. As we have seen, a specific characteristic of digital space is that its delimitations are inclusive rather than exclusive. An object that is in a box can be in another one at the same time. This is perhaps the most important difference between digital and non-digital space: the respective functions of the structures 'in' and 'out' do not work in the same way in both realms. The fundamental shift that this provokes in our system of values involves the interpretation of what is public and what is private.

In the first chapter, using the work of Beatriz Preciado, we examined how a particular architectural space can change family values. Playboy architecture, we observed, blurred the boundaries between in and out and thus posed a challenge to the middle-class family values of the 1950s. In digital space, these boundaries are even weaker. In all circumstances in digital space I am both 'in' and 'out', visible and invisible, public and private. This is why our way of defining our identity and dealing with other members of society has been subjected to radical change. It does not mean that there are *no* boundaries anymore, just that their meaning is no longer the same. We always manage to set boundaries and each boundary we set is dynamic and subject to being moved.

In the digital age, we are giving more and more importance to the separation between private and public, precisely because this separation is less and less stable. There is a simultaneous increase of attention to issues related to privacy in the public discourse with many academic and non-academic texts devoted to the topic,[62] and a dramatic rise of practices that cannot really be defined as either completely private or completely public. The difficulty of drawing a sharp line between private and public is one of the reasons why the web is a space of passwords – which clearly represent an attempt to separate spaces, including private spaces from public ones – and at the same time a space where the public and the private overlap. On the one hand, the web is a very compartmentalized space: each of its compartments represents a particular architectural framework, with its own accessibility and its own rules of visibility; on the other hand, these compartments are permeable. The web is thus both compartmentalized and fluid; it has many boundaries, but they are porous.

---

62   See, for example, David Lyon (ed.) *Surveillance as Social Sorting: Privacy, Risk, and Digital Discrimination*, London, New York: Routledge, 2003; Neil Richards, *Intellectual Privacy: Rethinking Civil Liberties in the Digital Age*, Oxford: Oxford University Press, 2014; Daniel J. Solove, *The Digital Person: Technology and Privacy in the Information Age*, New York: New York University Press, 2004.

A Facebook profile offers a clear manifestation of this paradox. Each profile is defined by an extensive set of rules that set out its delimitation: Facebook has various security systems that are dedicated to ensuring privacy: each user has a password and the site's algorithm tries to limit the accessibility of the profiles to only its owners. Also devices – especially personal ones, like phones or tablets – are designed to limit their use to only one user and even the discourse at times reflects this separation of private spaces: think 'personal' computer, for instance. A range of attributes that describe its accessibility and visibility characterizes each profile. We can use profile settings to make some information visible to everybody, some to only our closest friends, some to a different group of friends, some to friends of their friends, some to friend of friends of friends, and so on. From a certain angle, the whole platform seems conceived to give precedent to accessibility and privacy concerns: the privacy issue from this perspective can seem like the most important one. At the same time, we also get the feeling that every piece of information that appears on the site is potentially public, and this pushes us to believe that there are no boundaries anymore and that digital space is liquid and non-structured. This is not the case, though. The reason for the porosity of boundaries in digital space is not a lack of structure but rather an overlapping of different, and very well defined, structures. Private information is really quite private inside the space of a profile, but it is also quite accessible and public, if and when it is carried out this space. If somebody copies a picture from one profile and posts it to another one, this same picture is subjected to different criteria of accessibility and privacy. A picture that was initially visible only to my friends becomes visible to the friends of the new profile – or, if it is published in an open public space, to everyone. The digital picture is now in two different boxes at the same time, protected by two different levels of accessibility. This kind of simultaneity is quite difficult, if not impossible, for non-digital objects to achieve. Take the example of an old photograph that my mother keeps in the family album: it exists only in this album and it is subject only to the accessibility and privacy criteria of this album. One could copy the photo and multiply it – as Walter Benjamin showed in his essay *The Work of Art in the Age of its Technological Reproducibility* – but this would require a much greater effort than is needed to copy a digital picture. Still, the example illustrates the continuity of the change. Benjamin said that every work has always been reproducible: one could always go to the Louvre and make a copy of the Gioconda. But it is much easier to do so when the reproduction is aided by technology, as with a photograph. In the case of a digital object, the copy requires no effort at all: an object immediately exists in a multiple way and can be further multiplied without any effort. For example, the same file can be present in two different web pages, if you simply embed it: embedding means to visualize content in a page without actually copying it: the browser looks for the content on the server where it has been originally archived. But actually the file is on two – or more – different places at the same time. Another example: when we send a file as an attachment, we do not have to 'copy' it, but still we will have many manifestations of it. In this case, it is true that there is a copy (even many of them: one on the server of the sender, one on that of the receiver, one on the local directory of the sender, etc.), but this copy exists without any action or effort being needed. It shows that there is no original file anymore: the file on my laptop is exactly the same as the one on the computer of the receiver. This is why the delimitation criteria are inclusive.

All the spaces in which we live are characterized by this kind of delimitation. When I am home and inside the walls of my house, which frame a particular sort of privacy, this delimitation is well structured and clear: people outside the house cannot see me. But, if it is true that I am in a well defined space, it is also true that my body is at the same time a part of many other differently delimited spaces, like the space of my Skype contacts, or the space of the contacts of a friend of mine who is presently in my house, taking pictures and recording videos with his phone and sharing them with his contacts.

Delimitation in digital space implies a change of all the values linked with defining an inside and an outside, first of all of the relationship between public and private. From this we begin to understand that the entire construction of our identity is involved in this change: What is intimate? What is private? What is social? What groups do we belong to? And so on.

The inclusivity of delimitation in digital space leads to a multiplication of the positions that an object can occupy, and position is the spatial attribute on which all hierarchies are based. Spatial position tells us what is important and what is not, what is powerful and what is not, who has authority and who does not. The multiplication of possible positions means that there is not just one framework of positions; and, by extension, that there is not just one hierarchy. Things can be ordered using different hierarchical patterns and can be organized at the same time within multiple frameworks of power. The house at the periphery of the town – in non-digital space – is only at the periphery. It is not important on a hierarchical scale and it likely not the house of a rich and powerful family. The town's power is organized spatially within only one structure: the most central equals the most powerful. In digital space, however, an object can be, simultaneously, on the periphery of one spatial structure and in the center of another. This is what happens with the multiplication of online communities: each community has a different spatial structure and the relationships between its members are organized in a particular way. One person can belong to several different communities and thus can occupy several different positions and several different power positions.

This situation should not be considered as being completely dissimilar to the one that characterizes non-digital space. Even non-digital space, after all, allows for the overlapping of different spatial structures. Digital space facilitates such overlapping in particular, though, and makes it difficult to reduce overlapping structures to a single linear taxonomy. In non-digital space, a person could occupy a peripheral position in the social organization of a town but a central one in the organization of an association. This person would have little power in town but a great deal of power in the association. But it is easy to make a classification of these structures and to say that being central in a state is more important than being central in a town, or that being central in a town is more important than being central in an association. We can easily make a hierarchy of power and say, for instance, that the president of the United States is more important than the president of the association of the students of the literature department. This hierarchy of spatial structures is also possible in digital space: being first on the list of a Google results page, for example, is more important than topping the list of the internal search engine of a small site. But this kind of hierarchy is dynamic and can change very fast. A new small platform can become huge and can quickly acquire huge economic and political weight.

Non-digital space is characterized by the stabilization and institutionalization of spatial structures.

This stabilization can last for a very long time: years, decades, even centuries, if we think of states as spatial structures. In digital space, this stabilization is more ephemeral and so institutionalization is more complicated. It is premature to guess whether this characteristic is specific only to this early phase of digital culture and depends on the fact that digital spatial structures are quite new and have not yet had time to become institutionalized, or if it will remain a characteristic of digital culture even in the future.

The third aspect of spatial structures that we have talked about is the quantitative one, which refers to the distance between objects. Clearly, quantity is crucial in digital space: everything must be measurable – and measured. This implies that moral values are more and more associated with quantity. A page that has a more elevated PageRank is more interesting and is ultimately considered 'better'. The quality of everything is thus evaluated on the basis of its quantity: a restaurant with more reviews, a blog with more readers, a product with more buyers, a person with more friends. From this point of view, quality is not relevant: you do not have to know *who* has visited your site, only *how many* have. It is not important to know the tastes of the people reviewing a restaurant, just that many of them have found it good. An amusing anecdote can illustrate this point: in 2007, a ring was marketed that would display the number of Google results for the name of the person wearing the ring: it was called the Google Vanity Ring.[63] The idea behind the ring was that the more results a name received, the more worthy the person was – a calculation that was meant to suggest that the identity of a person was a measure of quantity.

This equivalence between quantity and quality is crucial in digital space because it is the basis of the functioning of computers. In order to classify something and to propose an organization of its contents, a computer must have numbers. But this idea is not new: it is a cultural *topos* that has traversed the history of thought, beginning with Pythagoras, moving through Descartes and Leibniz, and asserting itself in the last century in the thinking of advanced capitalism. The digital is only a clearer manifestation of this tendency.

Algorithms and Values

In order to understand more precisely the relationship between the structure of digital space and the values it produces, we will look at some examples. The question we should first address is: How can a specific spatial organization determine moral and political values. I will use the word 'platform' to define a particular online environment that has its own spatial organization. A platform can be a website, but also a more complex set of web pages and applications that are linked together and organized in a coherent way: Twitter, Google, Facebook, YouTube, Wikipedia, and so on can be talked about as platforms. Now, the foundation of the spatial structure of a platform is often an algorithm. This is the case for platforms like Google (PageRank) or Facebook or Amazon, or for all online dating systems,[64] for that

---

63   Laurent Bourrelly, 'Google Vanity Ring', *Observatoire Google*, 18 November 2007, http://google-observatoire.blogspot.it/2007/11/google-vanity-ring.html.

64   Marcello Vitali-Rosati, 'Les algorithmes de l'amour', in *MuseMedusa*, no. 2 (2014), http://musemedusa.com/dossier_2/marcello_vitali-rosati/.

matter. 'Code is law', as Lessig said in 2000:[65] the architecture of the code produces the rules that regulate our behaviors. But this also means that code creates values: it regulates our behavior according to certain principles – ethical, moral, and political.[66] This is another formulation of the theory of the nomos.

The best way to demonstrate this thesis would be to study, mathematically, the algorithms in question and try to understand which values they are based on and which values they suggest. But this approach is not possible for the simple reason that these algorithms are not public: we do not know the actual algorithms; we just know what the companies that made them tell us about them. Therefore, the only possible way to demonstrate the relationship between algorithms and values is to analyze the discourse surrounding them and not the algorithms themselves. This approach, even if it is not the most scientific one, is nonetheless useful. Our aim, after all, is not to learn how the spaces of these platforms are structured exactly, but rather the principles on which the structuring is made.

One could say that the public communications of these companies about their algorithms is more a form of advertising than a real description of them, and this is probably true. Still, for the purposes of understanding the values that a platform proposes, the discourse that emerges through advertising is not less interesting than the actual technical functioning of the platform.

Let us start by considering PageRank, which is probably one of the most influential algorithms in our daily lives. As Dominique Cardon argues (I translate):

> PageRank is a moral machine. It contains a system of values and gives the top position to the one that has been judged worthy. This expresses a particular will: to make the web a space where a merit system is neither limited nor deformed.[67]

'PageRank is a moral machine': this means both that it is based on certain moral principles – which pre-date it and that correspond to the convictions of its creators – and that it *creates* moral principles. Its algorithm represents a particular moral point of view and at the same time it produces one. As Brin and Page say in the first paper about Google,[68] PageRank is based on the academic citation system: the more a paper is cited, the more it is considered interesting. This structure – which obviously carries many ethical and political implications – is adapted to web pages: the more incoming links a page has, the higher its PageRank score and so the higher it ends up on the results list.

Obviously, this algorithm is based on a particular idea of meritocracy that produces a specific

65   Lawrence Lessig, *Code: And Other Laws of Cyberspace, Version 2.0*, New York: Basic Books, 2006.
66   T. Striphas, 'Algorithmic Culture', *European Journal of Cultural Studies* 18, no. 4-5 (2015): 395-412, doi:10.1177/1367549415577392.
67   Dominique Cardon, 'Dans l'esprit du PageRank', *Résaux*, vol. 177, nr. 1 (2013): 63-95, http://www.cairn.info/resume.php?ID_ARTICLE=RES_177_0063, p. 65.
68   Sergey Brin and Lawrence Page. 'The Anatomy of a Large-Scale Hypertextual Web Search Engine', *Computer Networks and ISDN Systems* 30, no. 1-7 (April 1998): 107-117, doi:10.1016/S0169-7552(98)00110-X.

conception of authority. The idea of citation analysis on which PageRank is based rests on a moral principle: we should evaluate the value of content by looking at the content itself rather than at who has produced it. Thus it is not the authority of the producer which gives value to the content – it is not because the content has been produced by a professor that it is more interesting or more true than content produced by a student. In such a system of values, the social hierarchy would be the basis of a content hierarchy. However, in a meritocracy as citation analysis understands it, it does not matter who produces content: the important criterion is whether or not it is worthy in itself. An idea that is clearly ideological. It does not remove the question of authority, but instead simply *moves* it: for how, exactly, should we evaluate the merit of content? How should one measure how interesting content is? The previously existing hierarchical system was a way of answering this question: authority was in place before the content was presented and so it functioned as a meter to measure the content's interest. In the meritocratic vision, the idea is that authority will emerge only after the appearance of the content itself; the content will establish authority and not the other way around. Or, to put it another way, in the hierarchical vision a paper is interesting because its author has authority; in the meritocratic system a paper has authority because it is interesting. But this description tells us nothing about how to evaluate the interest of a paper – or, in the case of the web, of a page.

The solution proposed by PageRank is a way of moving authority from a pre-established hierarchical structure to a calculation of quantity. The fact that interest is 'measured' with numbers gives the impression of a more objective evaluation: the meritocratic solution consists in counting the number of citations. This is a way of giving authority to a sort of collective intelligence, in which the judgment of the majority is the right one. It is no longer a social hierarchy, the thinking goes – where a professor is more reliable than a student – but rather a mass of people who belong to a community produces authority collectively: even authority is not really authority anymore – it is simply a product of merit. We no longer trust something because it has authority; it has an authority because it is reliable. And it is reliable because it is relied upon by others.

This is the underlying moral principle of PageRank. The idea, as I said, is built into the algorithm: the algorithm is conceived with a moral point of view and certain moral values. But, as Cardon shows, PageRank is also a moral machine, which means that it *produces* values. The most evident value is the objectivity of the machine: Google often insists on the fact that the results are not manually modified. The results are what the algorithm decides, without human intervention. This is meant to convey the idea that the meritocracy is completely 'objective'. The work of a machine is objective because the machine has no feelings that can interfere with its judgment. Google's classification is right, in other words, because it is based only on numbers.

The algorithm thus carries the value of a meritocracy based on two distinct ideas: one, that the most interesting content is the most cited; and two, that a machine is able to calculate this without being influenced by anything. This attention to the issue of objectivity is actually yet another way of criticizing a precedent system of authority: that is, a system in which authority comes from a person and is expressed through a person. This is why we 'feel' authority: it is based on a particular kind of personal relationship. Some people inspire authority; others do not. Now, a perfect meritocracy – as Google sees it – should be emancipated from any form of authority. There are no longer people behind the content. The algorithm judges only the links between documents, as if it were considering only the spatial structure of the network of documents and giving a bigger score to the documents that are more central in the network – because they are the most linked.

The discourse that Google asserts is that it replaces authority with meritocracy. But this is far from true. Basing the merit system on the number of citations is a way of granting authority to the majority and by extension recognizing a sort of distributed authority that expresses itself in the majority's thinking, which is materialized in the linked state of the content. It has been made clear that a spatial structure – involving a set of relationships between documents – determines how this authority expresses itself. One could say that this is not an authority in the proper sense because we can understand it. As Hannah Arendt insists, an authority is something we trust without being compelled by any reason. But if we analyze Google's PageRank meritocracy more carefully, we see that there is actually no reason to trust the citations analysis and that we don't really understand it. The idea that more linked pages should mean something pertinent is really only a kind of blind faith. Google simply analyzes the spatial structure of the web to discover in it an expression of authority, as was also possible in the case of the town's structure that we can study in order to gain an understanding of the different authorities operating within it. It is telling that the algorithm treats the most cited as the most important actors on the web: the fact that content is cited a lot does not really mean that the majority of people consider it interesting, but only that for some reason it is central in the network, perhaps because of the reputation or strength of a producer who already has high visibility – which would bring us back again to the person-based authority principle. The Matthew effect – Merton's idea that 'the rich get richer'[69] – applies here: content that is highly visible will be more often cited – and then *more* visible and *more* often cited. Google's system works because there are strong authority structures on the web that are understandable only if one looks at the spatial organization of contents. Another reason it works is because it is able to recognize these authorities by studying the structure of digital space, which involves relationships between the objects. The ability to understand this structure may ultimately be the source of Google's authority. The average user – who does not know how PageRank works – simply recognizes Google as an authority: content is interesting because it is first on Google's results page.

Another example that illustrates how algorithms carry moral values is found in Online Dating Systems (ODS) – in particular, those that are based on the idea that users can find 'true love' – sites like Match.com or OkCupid. A question that scholars have tried to answer is whether or not it is possible to find love with these ODS. This has involved questioning the efficiency of algorithms: can an algorithm work so well as to be able to make love happen? This kind of question is based on the idea that digital technologies are tools that allow us (effectively or not) to do things that we have tried to do also without digital technologies. For instance, human beings have always travelled, but the speed of travel has increased thanks to cars and planes. As we discussed earlier, however, this way of thinking is flawed: in fact, cars and planes do not only make something that we already did faster; they completely change

---

69   Robert Merton, 'The Matthew Effect in Science', *Science* 159, no. 3810 (1968): 56-63.

our perception of space – and not only in a quantitative way. All the relationships between towns and regions are shaped by transportation – if it exists or not, if it is cheap or not, if it is frequent, or comfortable, etc. The hierarchy of towns is reshaped; their accessibility and their distances are modified. In the same way, the algorithms of ODS do not enable us to find love more quickly: they change our very conception of love.

Thus we can say, paraphrasing Cardon, that ODS algorithms are moral machines because they produce an idea of love that leads users to harbour specific expectations of what they may actually find when dating online. As with PageRank, ODS algorithms are based on pre-existing values, and at the same time they produce values. In another work I showed that ODS start from a familiar or conventional idea of romantic love which it transforms by adding the idea of control:[70] you are not passive in your love life, you can take control of it thanks to this algorithm. Once again, we encounter the myth of the power and the objectivity of calculation.

If we read the presentation of one of the most widely used ODS, Match.com, we can easily identify the conception of love that it is proposing. On the home page of the platform we read:

Every year, hundreds of thousands of people find love on Match.com. Match.com pioneered the Internet dating industry, launching in 1995 and today serves millions of singles in 24 countries. Match.com continues to *redefine* the way single men and single women meet, flirt, date and fall in love, proving time and again that you can *make love happen* through on-line dating and that *lasting relationships* are possible. Match.com singles are *serious about finding love.* And Match puts you in *control* of your love life; meeting that *special someone* and forming a *lasting* relationship is as *easy* as clicking on any one of the photos and singles ads available on-line.[71] (my italics)

There are several important aspects of this presentation to take note of. The first is that the ODS wants to *redefine* what it means to meet someone and fall in love. A familiar listing of the essential attributes of love emerges from this quote, the sorts of things that we would find in a blockbuster romantic movie: love is about destiny, about finding your soul mate, the only person in the world for you, and it is something magical and irrational. How does it happen? Why? Nobody can say. Match.com allows users to look at millions of profiles and this enables them to find that special person they are destined for, even if that person lives far away (they company advertises that it serves 24 countries). The algorithm produces this magic – which would be impossible without the calculating power of the machine. At the same time, we cannot accept the idea that love is created by a mechanical calculation: it would be too rationally deterministic and love cannot be reduced to a destiny that is so cold and squared. This is why, on the Match.com homepage, love is presented as something that *happens*. So it also produces itself in a magical way. The cold calculation of the algorithm contains an element of magic, largely because it is very complicated and users are unable to understand how it works: like love itself. Mathematics has always had

70   Vitali-Rosati, 'Les algorithmes de l'amour'.
71   See, *http://www.match.com*, visited on 18 July 2017.

a magical aspect and the fact that an algorithm is able find the right person for anyone gives a mysterious power.

These two characteristics, destiny and magic, have infused our understanding of love since the Middle Ages. But the description of love on Match.com proposes something more: the idea of control. Love is presented as something serious; it must last. Love happens, but we can regain control of it and be the masters of our love lives. This element of control, according to the site's presentation text, allows us to have stability in love. Love is presented as something serious; it must last. The algorithm enables control over something that has always been conceived as uncontrollable. The desire to maintain control, especially over things that appear to be beyond our control, is a recurring dream in the history of humanities. Digital culture articulates this dream in a new way with the myth of calculability. Everything that is calculable is controllable.

A Hybrid Space

Exactly what kind of space is digital space? How can we summarize its characteristics? And what is its relationship with other, non-digital, spaces? Following the analysis above, we can identify three characteristics of digital space:

1. Digital space is our actual space. The adjective 'digital' is used to refer to the very space in which we are living today. The adjective cannot be limited to technologies: it has acquired a cultural meaning that captures a set of characteristics, structures, and values that describes our society. Digital space is the space of digital society. For this reason, it should not be considered a parallel space: it is the only space we inhabit today. Hence, digital space cannot be considered as immaterial, or inauthentic, or fictive. The virtuality of digital space is a characteristic of every space because a space is always a sort of virtualization.

2. Digital space is different from other spaces such as, the space of pre-digital societies in degree and not in quality. All the characteristics of digital space existed before, if to a different degree. For instance, the possibility of multiplying the positions of an object – the position of a book in a library, for example – characterizes every space, but this possibility is more prominent in digital space. In this respect, there is no rupture between digital space and pre-digital spaces. There has not been a revolution, only a continuous change. Digital space shares with all other spaces certain primary characteristics: it is a set of relationships between objects, it is made of writing, it exists in the context of actions, it produces values, and it leads to a particular form of authority.

3. Digital space is a hybrid space. The continuity between pre-digital spaces and digital space implies that digital space is a hybridization of ancient and new characteristics. Some structures of pre-digital spaces are present in digital space and others have been altered – although in degree and not in quality. In the next chapter we will see that this is the reason why some ancient forms of authority continue to operate in digital space. Once again, the emergence of the digital does not imply a revolution. There is no rupture between pre-digital and digital space.

To conclude, digital space is a space like all the other spaces: it is, foremost, a set of relationships between objects. Next we will analyze how this set of relationships is organized, as we could with any other space like the space of the modern society or the space of the medieval city. The particular organization that is specific to digital space we will call 'editorialization'.

4. EDITORIALIZATION

A History of the Term

The word 'editorialization', in the sense that it is used here, is a neologism in English. It comes from the French *éditorialisation*. In English the word is a derivative of editorialize, which means – according to most dictionaries[72] – 'to express an opinion in the form of an editorial' or 'to introduce opinion into the reporting of facts'. In French the word has acquired a broader meaning and is related in particular to digital culture and to digital forms of producing knowledge. This shift in meaning, from an idea that denotes the expression of opinion to one that suggests the production of knowledge in the digital age, is actually quite useful and not particularly problematic; as we will see, the digital version of the term retains its association with the notion of opinion in that it refers to the production of content that expresses a kind of opinion or that offers a better way to see or interpret the world.

A redefinition of this concept can also be very useful as a way of interpreting and understanding the structure of digital space and, by extension, the forms of authority that are found in it. More than a simple concept, editorialization is a comprehensive theory. Before exploring the meaning of the term and the theoretical framework it sets, it is necessary to provide some history of the word in the French research community.

Since 2007, the word éditorialisation has been used more and more in French, but it is sometimes very difficult to understand precisely the sense in which scholars adopt the term, and even more difficult to track its usage in the last ten years. In 2004, Brigitte Guyot used the term to refer both to the devices that enable mediation between information and their users and to the process of information mediation itself. She writes:

> When a mediation device is involved in the first relationship between a piece of information and the one who uses it, an organizational order appears. There is a construction, an "editorialization" that introduces mediation, but also a distance that is produced by the fact that an intellectual system (all the operations of translation and interpretation) and an organizational system (which manages accessibility and relationship modalities) are created.[73]

In this sense, editorialization becomes almost a synonym of 'mediation'. The problem is that, in the formulation of Guyot, one could make the mistake of imagining that a non-mediated relationship with information is possible, which is clearly not the case, as the work of McLuhan and his disciples in media studies made clear. That Guyot's recognized the problematic use of the word is demonstrated by the fact that she removed it from the final version of her 2004 paper.

---

72   See for example Collins, http://www.collinsdictionary.com/dictionary/english/editorialize, Merriam-Webster, http://www.merriam-webster.com/dictionary/editorialize, or Cambridge http://dictionary.cambridge.org/us/dictionary/english/editorialize.

73   Brigitte Guyot, *Sciences de l'information et activité professionnelle*, vol. 38, C.N.R.S. Editions, 2004, http://www.cairn.info/resume.php?ID_ARTICLE=HERM_038_0038. Translation by the author.

Bruno Bachimont outlined the concept of editorialization for the first time in 2007. He discusses the move towards indexation in what he refers to as 'editorialization':

> The central idea of this article is that the indexing of digital content introduces a new relationship between content and document. While in traditional indexing the challenge is to find the document containing the information that is sought, digital content indexing enables the finding of segments involved in the search for information and configures these segments. If the document is present in the search results in traditional indexing and searching, it is not the same in digital indexing. In the latter type of indexing, the segments can dissociate from the content from which they are derived, losing their origin and documentary nature. By becoming resources, these segments are remobilized for the production of other content. The goal is no longer to find documents but to produce new ones using available resources. One thus moves away from indexing for research in favor of indexing for publication. Since the latter is carried out according to certain standards and norms, editorialization enables indexed segments to be enlisted in the editorial process for new publications.[74]

The concept of editorialization here serves to describe an editorial activity that is based on the indexed fragments of a document. Bachimont employs editorialization to explain an important shift: that of a non-digital document to a digital document. This shift consists of a transfer of information, which is restructured in order to be adapted to a digital environment. The term is thus used to explain the necessity of adapting non-digital content to a digital environment. Bachimont's use of the word implies the following characteristics:

- A deep link between editing activity and the practice of producing content in the digital realm.
- An element of fragmentation in the digital production of content.
- The necessity of recontextualization in adapting non-digital content to a digital environment.

Due to increasing digital editorial activity in recent years, the concept of editorialization has had great success and has been employed by many scholars and many actors in digital publishing. In particular Gérard Wormser, the director of the electronic journal *Sens public*,[75] began using 'editorialization' in 2008 to characterize the very peculiar activity of the journal and its network. One of the purposes of the research developed in *Sens public*'s network was – and still is – to study the impact of digital technology on the circulation of knowledge. This study was both theoretical and practical: it was the topic of many papers published in the journal, and it was also at the center of the very organization of the journal. *Sens public* was born in 2003 with the goal of renewing intellectual and academic exchanges with the purpose of taking advantage of the network possibilities produced by the web. *Sens public* is thus not only a journal but a network of individuals scattered across the globe, a thematic

---

74   Bruno Bachimont, 'Nouvelles tendances applicatives: de l'indexation à l'éditorialisation', in *L'indexation multimédia*, Paris: Hermès, 2007, http://cours.ebsi.umontreal.ca/sci6116/Ressources_files/BachimontFormatHerme%CC%80s.pdf. Translation by the author.

75   See http://sens-public.org.

network – sometimes with differing interests – a network of ideas and practices.[76] The concept of editorialization seems to be the most accurate way of describing what happens at *Sens public*. In 2008, it was clear that the publishing process – in the sense that it is used in traditional academic journals – was at work at *Sens public*, yet not everything being done could be described as publishing, at least not in the traditional sense of the term. One cannot, for instance, discuss digital publishing without addressing the differences between printed and digital practices, and these differences must somehow be thoroughly addressed. Another thing is that the particular role of the network of individuals behind the journal was very different from the network of an editorial board. Editorialization, first and foremost, addresses these differences: it consists in editorial practices that cannot be lumped together with what we generally refer to as 'editing' or 'publishing'.

In order to structure the work on the new forms of production and circulation of knowledge in the digital environment, Gérard Wormser and I established a research laboratory at the Maison des sciences de l'homme Paris-Nord in 2008. The name Wormser proposed for the laboratory was: 'Pratiques interdisciplinaires et circulation du savoir: vers une éditorialisation des SHS' (Interdisciplinary practices and the circulation of knowledge: towards an editorialization of human and social sciences). In our request for the establishment of the MSH laboratory, we wrote (I translate):

> It is important to understand how the aesthetics of new media and cognitive technologies are redefining practices and to share the outcomes of this transformation. The concept of editorialization is characterized by the articulation of content production, technical and communicative factors, and the dynamics of contemporary exchanges in the humanities. This question branches across a range of accessible media and all of their records: accessibility, objectivity, legibility, comprehensiveness, tone, document structuring, links (...) How should we think about the encyclopedia of digital knowledge?

We used the term editorialization in a broad sense, to describe any digital editorial activity as well as any activity that is native to digital space. Two aspects of this appropriation of the term were derived from Bachimont's initial definition:

- The fact that the digital editorial gesture has its own specificity: techniques condition the structuring of thought.
- The fact that there is a fragmentation of the editorial gesture in digital space: there is a complex relationship between fragment and the rearrangement of fragments in units of meaning.

Moving from these aspects, the concept began to take on a broader meaning: it helped illuminate how knowledge is produced in the digital age in general. This shift to a broader meaning correlates to the cultural implication of the word 'digital' discussed in the previous chapter. If 'the digital' is not only about tools but in fact refers to a whole cultural environment, then editorialization – the way of producing contents in digital environments – must have a cultural dimension as well.

---

76   Marcello Vitali-Rosati, 'Les revues littéraires en ligne: entre éditorialisation et réseaux d'intelligences', in *Études françaises* 50, no. 3 (2014): 83, doi:10.7202/1027191ar.

In other words, the difference between publishing and editorialization is not only a difference of tools, but rather signifies a broader cultural difference: editorialization is not the way we produce knowledge using digital tools; it is the way we produce knowledge in the age of the digital, or, better, in digital society. In this sense, the term editorialization expresses an idea quite close to the notion of 'knowledge design' as it has been defined by Jeffrey Schnapp.[77]

Since 2008 the term has been used increasingly in France and in the francophone research community. I created a permanent international workshop (Digital Writing and Editorialization) to which – over the years – most of the scholars working on the topic have contributed, and the term editorialization has become an institutional concept. I have dedicated many papers to a definition of the concept.[78] In April 2015, Jérôme Valluy completed an almost exhaustive bibliographical work on the term, finding more than seventy academic papers that had used it.[79] Still, in spite of its success, the term's exact meaning has not yet been well defined. I will propose here an analysis of the different meanings of editorialization and examine the relationships between them.

What is Editorialization?

We can identify three different definitions of editorialization: a restrictive definition, a more general definition, and a third definition that tries to combine the first two.[80] According to a restrictive definition, editorialization is a set of technical devices (networks, servers, platforms, CMS, search engine algorithms), structures (hypertext, multimedia, metadata), and practices (annotation, comments, recommendations via social networks) that produces, organizes, and enables the circulation of content on the web.[81] In other words, editorialization is the process of producing and diffusing content in a digital environment. We could say that, in this sense, editorialization is what publishing becomes under the influence of digital technologies. Obviously, this has an impact on the content itself: the concept of editorialization tries to stress how technology shapes content. Defined in this way, one could say editorialization can be identified with content curation, or digital curation – which is the process of organizing content in a particular digital environment. But there is a crucial difference: the concept of editorialization has a cultural dimension that is not present in content curation. Content curation is the practice of collecting, organizing, and displaying content in a particular environment. On the contrary, editorialization refers to how tools, emerging practices, and the structures determined by the tools engender a different relationship to the content itself. We could say that curation is

---

77 Jeffrey Schnapp, 'Knowledge Design', 2011, http://jeffreyschnapp.com/wp-content/uploads/2011/06/HH_lectures_Schnapp_01.pdf.
78 Marcello Vitali-Rosati, 'Digital Paratext'; Vitali-Rosati, 'Les revues littéraires en ligne'; Marcello Vitali-Rosati, 'What Is Editorialization ?' *Sens public*, 4 January 2016, http://sens-public.org/article1059.html.
79 Jérome Valluy, '"Editorialisation" (recherche bibliographique, Avril 2015)', *Terra-HN*, 2015, http://www.reseau-terra.eu/article1333.html.
80 Roberto Gac has underlined the existence of these two definitions in 'Éditorialisation et littérature: du roman à l'intertexte', 18 March 2016, *Sens public*, http://www.sens-public.org/article1185.html?lang=fr.
81 Vitali-Rosati, 'Digital Paratext'.

the action of a specific individual or defined group, whereas editorialization refers to the way this action is shaped by the characteristics of the digital environment. We should underline that these characteristics are not only technical but cultural.

Let us consider an example in order to better grasp this first definition. Imagine we have medical information about a particular disease – let us say, avian influenza. We have a description of the disease and its history, we have data about pandemics, we have a list of the influenza's types, we have statistics about mortality, and we have advice for people to prevent contamination. A government could decide to create a platform to provide citizens with this information. For this purpose, a group of experts starts to curate all the content: they edit the texts and adapt them to the target public, they choose a way to display the data (graphics, tables, etc.), they structure the platform and work on its ergonomics, and perhaps they also create Twitter and Facebook accounts to promote the platform and to communicate about it. All these actions fall into the category of what we would call curation. The platform will have users; they interact with it, comment on its information, and possibly relay content on their social networks. They will likely reuse some of the information on other platforms, and they post the link of the platform on other sites. The platform is indexed by search engines, and algorithms rank it in order to put it on a hierarchical list. The platform as such occupies a particular position on the web: a symbolic position – less or more visible, or important, or reliable. These aspects will evolve over a course of days and weeks and months and years. This is editorialization. The accumulation of all these elements is what produces the content and gives it its meaning. We could say that curation is a part of editorialization and that editorial-ization is the whole process, that it takes into account everything that is involved in the production of the cultural meaning of content.

Thus editorialization shapes and structures content in a way that is not limited to a closed, well-defined context (such as a journal) or a group of predetermined individuals (editors and publishers). It involves an opening up of space (several platforms) and time (several different editors unbound by deadlines). This opening up is one of the key differences between curation and editorialization. It is also what distinguishes editorialization from publishing. The opening up of editorialization in relation to printed editing involves a certain loss of control on the part of the writer, editor, or publisher with respect to content. The writer, editor, and publisher become only a part of an editorial process that itself is much larger in scope.

Let us consider another example: the publication of an academic paper. The editorial team of an online journal works on the editing of the paper and publishes it. They correct the text, format it, mark it up (in html or xml, for instance), edit metadata, and finally publish it on the journal platform. This work is quite the same as editing for traditional print. But in the digital environment this is only the beginning of the process. The life of the paper, its visibility, and its circulation depend on a more complex structure, which involves comments, citations, re-use (including plagiarism), and indexation. This is out of the control of the editing team. For example, if Google puts the paper on the top of a results list, this is an important development that is comparable to the paper being put on the cover of a printed journal and the journal being placed in the window of a bookshop. We could say that there are uncontrolled aspects for the printed edition as well – being put in a bookshop window, for instance, is not the choice of the writer, editor, or publisher – but the degree of control has clearly changed in digital space.

The obvious limitation of this first definition is that it considers the digital environment as a discrete, separated space. In this sense it is a web-centered definition that does not take into consideration the fluidity that exists between digital and pre-digital space.[82] The second definition is an extension of the first and is based on the assumption that digital space determines an overlapping and ultimately a fusion between discourse and reality. I will explain this idea in detail later, but for the moment it is sufficient to understand the basic outlines: in the digitally connected world, to exist is to be editorialized. In digital space, an object must be connected and positioned in order for it to exist. For example, for a restaurant to exist, it has to be on TripAdvisor or on Google Maps or on some other platform that gives it a position and makes it visible and comprehensible. In order for a person to exist in digital space, they have to be a profile on Facebook, Twitter, LinkedIn, or some other platform that classifies the person or makes them visible. Editorialization is the condition for this existence. Now, if this is true, editorializing means not only producing content but also producing reality itself. According to this very broad definition, editorialization is a set of collective forms of negotiating reality. In other words, editorialization is the set of social practices that leads us to understand, organize, and judge the world. The fact that the space we live in is digital space, suggests that all these practices take place in digital space, which means that every practice tending towards an understanding, organization, or judgment of the world is an act of editorialization.

The problem with this second definition is that it is too general and too broad. It is difficult to imagine something that, in this broader sense, is not editorialization. The definition therefore risks becoming meaningless. Further analysis shows that these two definitions can be fused in order to create a more efficient and operational definition. We can take all the acts of structuring content online – on the web or on other forms of the connected environment, like mobile apps – and consider these acts in their function of shaping our whole reality. In this sense, we can define editorialization as a set of individual and collective actions that take place in a digital online environment and that aim to structure the way we understand, organize, and judge the world. These actions are shaped by the digital environment in which they take place, and so editorialization, just as the first definition makes clear, is not only about what people do but also how their actions are shaped and oriented by a particular environment. But the emphasis needs to be put not only on how we produce content, but also on the fact that these contents are actually the world in which we live. It is important to stress that, if we consider the word digital in a cultural sense, as we did in the first chapter, digital space is our primary space, the space in which we live. With this in mind, we can make a distinction between various digital environments – for instance, the web and other

---

82   For a discussion on the relationship between digital and non-digital space in academic publications, see Daniel Paul O'Donnell, 'A "Thought Piece" on Digital Space as Simulation and the Loss of the Original', *dpod blog*, 11 February 2015, http://dpod.kakelbont.ca/2015/02/11/a-thought-piece-on-digital-space-as-simulation-and-the-loss-of-the-original/.

forms of connected environment – and digital space as a hybridization of these environments with the totality of our world. These considerations allow us to further modify our definition and to arrive at a final one:

Editorialization is the set of dynamics that produce and structure digital space. These dynamics can be understood as the interactions of individual and collective actions within a particular digital environment.

The object of editorialization is not content, but the world itself: we editorialize things, or, better, we editorialize the space in which we live. We could say that the encyclopedic project as it was conceived during the 18th century by Diderot and D'Alambert was realized with the world wide web: the totality of our knowledge has been organized and linked in a unique and huge architectural framework.[83] But it goes further: with editorialization we are not only structuring the knowledge, we are structuring the world itself. We can say that editorialization is not only an architecture of knowledge (or, to use Schnapp's concept, a 'knowledge design') but more precisely an architecture of being. This is why the concept of space becomes so crucial: editorialization is a way of organizing space not in a metaphorical sense (as the space of knowledge or the space of information): editorialization is an actual architectural action, it organizes our actual space.

This definition implies three aspects of editorialization that we should consider: a technological one, a cultural one and a practical one. It is crucial to understand that editorialization has a relationship with a 'particular digital environment', which means that editorialization is somehow related to specific technologies. The term editorialization was created in part as a way of understanding the impact of technology on the production of content, and one aspect of this is the fact that devices, digital platforms, tools, networks, and protocols simultaneously provide the context of the content and act as the elements that structure this content. This phenomenon has been studied by many scholars and defined, for example, as 'affordance'[84] or interpreted as technological determinism.[85] The same consideration of the technological impact on content can be made for all content production and circulation technologies, also historical ones.[86] The digital environment is prescriptive in the sense that it determines the form of the content it can host. This means that the technological dimension is crucial for editorialization. At the same time, editorialization should not be reduced to a question of technology.

Indeed, there exists a very complex relationship between technology and culture, which is why the cultural dimension is also crucial to our definition of editorialization. Certainly, when trying to understand the structure of digital space, it is important to avoid falling into what

---

83   For an analysis of the relationship between the *Encyclopédie* and the structure of digital space, see Benoît Melançon, 'Sommes-nous les premiers lecteurs de l'Encyclopédie?', in Jean-Michel Salaün et Christian Vandendorpe (eds) *Les Défis de la publication sur le Web : hyperlectures, cybertextes et méta-éditions*, pp. 145-65. Lyon: ENSSIB, 2004.

84   Donald A. Norman, *The Design of Everyday Things*, New York: Basic Books, 2002.

85   Friedrich Kittler, *Optical Media*, Cambridge, UK, Malden, Mass.: Polity, 2009.

86   See for example, Michael Warner, *The Letters of the Republic: Publication and the Public Sphere in Eighteenth-Century America*, Cambridge, Mass.: Harvard University Press, 1992.

has been called 'technological determinism',[87] the view that technology's development is something almost mechanical – a progression – that it determines cultural change. As we showed in the first chapter, however, culture and technology are bound in something like a circular relationship: the convergence of certain cultural ideas and technological advances brings about change, and this change is in turn affected by both cultural and technological elements. Or, to put it in simpler language: culture influences technology, and technology influences culture. It is quite impossible to separate these two processes. Thus editorialization also describes the ways our cultural traditions influence our ways of structuring content.

Take the example of hypertext. The idea of hypertext existed before the development of the web. It is well known that Vannevar Bush talked about the idea in 1945,[88] that Nelson later adapted Bush's idea to informatics,[89] and that, finally, Tim Berners-Lee was inspired by the idea when he conceived HTML. We could go even further back in time to find the idea of non-linear classification of content. It was present already in the first library classification systems, in the 3rd century BC. The catalogues in the Library of Alexandria, for instance, used a key-word classification system.[90] So, without some understanding of the cultural history of non-linear classification, we will be unable to understand hypertextual structure in its particular technological manifestation, HTML.

The third aspect of editorialization is the practical one, which takes into account the fact that technological and cultural structures need practices in order to be actualized. Technological possibility and cultural tradition are not enough in themselves. If no one creates and uses hypertexts, then hypertexts would not exist. At the same time, practices are not simply applications of cultural and technological possibilities: practices are creative. This element underlines the crucial importance of collectivity in the editorialization process. The different forms of editorialization depend on the fact that specific actions become common – which means that groups of people begin doing them and they become practice. Consider the example of the hashtag. The action of putting a # before a word in the Twitter environment is a way of designating the word a keyword. This action was not predicted by the platform. Twitter was not conceived to manage keywords. Somebody began doing this, and then a group of people began doing the same thing, and then it became a practice. This practice obliged Twitter to adapt its platform to take into account the keywords – what we now refer to as 'hashtags'. In other words, the practice influences the technology and shapes it, and – as the history of keywords clearly demonstrates – practices have a cultural background. In this way, the three aspects of editorialization – the technological, the cultural, and the practical – are merged. They can only theoretically be separated.

---

87   Ralph Schroeder, *Rethinking Science, Technology, and Social Change*, Stanford: Stanford University Press, 2007.

88   Vannevar Bush, 'As We May Think', *Atlantic Magazine*, July 1945, http://www.theatlantic.com/magazine/archive/1945/07/as-we-may-think/303881/.

89   T.H. Nelson, 'Complex Information Processing: A File Structure for the Complex, the Changing and the Indeterminate', in *Proceedings of the 1965 20th National Conference*, ACM '65, New York: ACM, 1965, doi:10.1145/800197.806036.

90   Doueihi, *Pour un humanisme numérique*.

The Processual Nature of Editorialization

In order to understand the peculiar nature of editorialization and to identify the characteristics that distinguish it from other manners of structuring content, we will analyze its attributes. There are five main attributes that constitute editorialization: the processual, the performative, the ontological, the multiple, and the collective.

First of all, editorialization is a process; more precisely, it is an open process. Editorialization is a series of actions in movement without a well-defined beginning or end. Each editorialization process is always in progress; it is always in dynamic motion. The processual nature of editorialization implies that it is very difficult to identify and isolate a single act of editorialization: every editorialization is in some way related to others, and it is impossible to sharply delimit a precise chain of actions. Let us consider again the example of the publication of an academic paper in an online journal. We could say that this example provides us with an *a fortiori* argument: if we can establish that the online publication of an academic paper is an open process, then logic will dictate that all other forms of editorialization are open processes.

The editorial process of publishing an academic paper in a printed journal can to some extent be defined and isolated according to the people who function in the process: there is an author who writes the paper, the journal's editorial board, probably two or three reviewers, and finally a group of people working for the publishing house that publishes the journal. We could count these people: there may be more of them (in the case of a big journal) or less (in the case of a little one), but the number will in any case be precise. The editorial process begins when the paper is proposed for publication by the author, and it ends when the journal is printed. Once the journal is printed, the paper is something that is stable and static. One could argue that the distribution of the journal, the reactions of its readers, and the number of citations it receives, etc. are also very important and should be considered as part of the editorial process. Although this is certainly true, it is also undeniable that the crucial moment of the printing signifies a discontinuity in the process: the paper will remain exactly as it appears at that moment.

In the case of an online paper, identifying its publication as an isolated and defined process is either more difficult or very arbitrary – if not to say impossible. Let us consider the process from the moment the author has finished the paper and proposes it for publication. (We will set aside the writing phase for the moment.) The beginning of the process is quite similar to that of a publication in a printed journal: there is an editorial board that is well-defined and composed of a precise number of persons, probably two or three reviewers, and a group of people who format the paper and publish it on the online platform. But the process is not finished at this point. First of all, the place the paper occupies is not yet decided. In a printed journal, the editor would decide where the paper will appear: in what position in the journal, on what pages, whether it will be on the cover or not. For an online paper, its position – and ultimately its meaning – also depends on a set of factors that are external to the editorial group: the position it will occupy on a search engine results list, for instance. If, in the printed publication, relationships between different papers are proposed by the editor – who has purposely put certain material together in the same printed journal – in the case of an online paper, the relationships are created by other platforms, which aggregate the contents. The paper is accessible from the website of the journal itself, through its index or archive, but it is also accessible from a list of results on Google Search: the search engine becomes another index. The electronic journal aggregator Project MUSE indexes the paper too, and places it on keywords-based lists. The paper can be quoted and cited on several networks such as Twitter or Academia, and a conversation about it can take place within the online community. The paper becomes a part of different wholes and each of them gives to it a different meaning. The overall meaning of the paper is the result of all these interactions together. Of course, the same structure of diffusion and commentary exists for the printed papers, but in the digital environment these structures become a part of the paper itself, because they exist in the very same space as the paper. In the printed journal, following Genette's analysis,[91] one could distinguish between the text and the epitext because the epitext belonged to another space – another book or another journal. In the case of a digital paper, however, the commentary, the results list, and the social network recommendation are all in the same space: on the web. They become a part of the paper itself.

Moreover, the paper is not fixed like a printed paper that is impossible to change unless one produces a second edition. The digital paper can easily be changed or copied and re-used in other contexts. Even if the editor tries to limit these kinds of practices, they are part of the very nature of digital environment: copying demands no effort and thus becomes a common practice. The paper can therefore be present in different forms in different places. For example, the practice of publishing a version of a paper for an institutional archive is more and more accepted. The life of the paper continues after the end of the editors' work, and the editors have no more control over it. The editorial process is open both in space and in time: in space because it is not limited to a specific platform or to a specific group of persons – as was the case with the printed version – and in time because there is no single moment when the movement of the paper stops, as there is with the moment of printing.

In fact, even the beginning of the process – the writing phase – is more open. The author may have a blog, and the work on the paper could start with a first intuition written on a blog post. The author might receive comments from colleagues or friends or readers, reading suggestions and other information, and further discussion. The work of writing the paper in that way turns out to be an editorialization process as well.

The result of these developments is multi-layered instability: the journal is no longer a stable form of circulation[92] because access to a paper does not depend on the journal but rather on other platforms, like a search engine or a social network; and the paper itself becomes an unstable object that can be subject to fragmentation: one can extract data from a paper and consider the data as original units that can be aggregated in many different ways.[93] The processual nature of editorialization is thus very deeply related to the idea of fragmentation that was first underlined by Bachimont.

---

91 Gérard Genette, *Seuils*.

92 Vitali-Rosati, 'Les revues littéraires en ligne'.

93 Niels Stern, Jean-Claude Guédon, and Thomas Wiben Jensen, 'Crystals of Knowledge Production: An Intercontinental Conversation about Open Science and the Humanities', *Nordic Perspectives on Open Science* 1 (2015): 1, doi:10.7557/11.3619.

To an extent these qualities characterize the printed edition as well. But again, this is in keeping with the main thesis of this book: there is no digital revolution, because digital culture is in continuity with pre-digital culture. The differences are more a question of degree than of quality. The cultural tendencies that we are witnessing now are tendencies that can be traced through the history of cultures. They are not completely new. The processual element that characterizes digital culture is a case in point: it was there already in printed culture, although that insisted on the possibility of controlling a well-defined and delimited process.

The Performative Nature of Editorialization

The concept of performativity has had an important theoretical impact in recent decades. Beginning with Austin's work on the speech act,[94] moving on to performance studies in the field of theater,[95] and arriving at the application of performativity to the field of gender studies,[96] the definition of the concept has varied according to the context in which it has been used. For this reason, it is almost impossible to provide a definition of performance or performativity that everyone can agree on. For the purposes of this chapter, performativity will be defined as the normative aspect of an action. Every action can be observed either by focusing on the aspects that determine it – its context, the constraints involved, etc. – or by focusing on its undecided aspect – how it is new, how it produces something that was not previously decided upon. The quality of performativity refers to the fact that a particular action produces something that was not predicted – was not predictable – before the action itself. In this sense, the notion of performativity denotes an approach to reality that does not focus on the essence of things and that rejects the paradigm of representation. I am aware that this definition is a simplification of a very complex subject, but for the purposes of this chapter it is will suffice.

Editorialization is performative for two main reasons: first, it is a process that does not follow a pre-defined scheme; and second, it does not represent reality but produces it. Editorialization is thus an open process. This is one of the main differences between editorialization and the printed edition. The open aspect of editorialization is in sharp contrast to the printing tradition, where an established protocol has to be followed, one that is decided upon before the editing and publishing process begins. With editorialization there is no protocol and the different steps are decided one-by-one. At the same time, a particular editorialization process can become normative, which means that it can become a model for other processes. Editorialization creates its own norms in a performative way. One may object that digital platforms predetermine the process: the act of posting photos on Facebook in some way reflects the degree to which Facebook determines behavior and even the whole process of publication. This is obviously true, but it is also true that alternative uses of the platform remain possible and that it is sometimes very easy to get around the schema imposed by the platform. The Twitter hashtag is a clear example of the performativity of editorialization: the process takes a particular form that was not predicted nor predictable, and this form then becomes a norm.

---

94   Austin, John Langshaw, and James Opie Urmson, *How to Do Things with Words: The William James Lectures Delivered at Harvard University in 1955*, Cambridge, Mass: Harvard University Press, 2009.
95   Richard Schechner, *Performance Theory*, London: Routledge, 2009.
96   Judith Butler, *Excitable Speech: A Politics of the Performative*, New York: Routledge, 1997.

Another example is provided by literary profiles on Facebook – we will analyze this case in the last chapter of this book.

The other element of editorialization that places it in a performative paradigm is its operational nature. Editorialization is a performative act in the sense that it tends to operate on reality rather than represent it. We read and we write in digital space – and in particular on the web – but most of the time this reading and writing has a precise operational purpose. This is the reason why editorialization in not a way of organizing knowledge – an architecture of information – but more precisely a way of organizing the world itself – an architecture of being. When we are organizing a trip and we buy plane tickets on Expedia, for instance, we are writing something – the names of the departure city and of the arrival city, a travel schedule, our preferences – and in this writing aim to do something: the writing aims to realize the travel. The written page created on Expedia – the page where the itinerary is presented, with all the information about the journey – has a distinctly performative quality: the document itself produces the travel and not only information about the travel.

One could object that this is a very specific example that is not representative of most of our (digital) reading and writing practices, but there are numerous less obvious examples of how editorialization fits a performative paradigm.

Take the example of a review on TripAdvisor. We could locate this action in a representational paradigm: the review represents the restaurant. In keeping with the paradigm, we have a signifier (the review) and a signified (the restaurant) – or, using the same paradigm, a sense and a reference.[97] But this interpretation does not truly reflect the reality of the reviewing practice. In writing a review, one *produces* the restaurant and contributes to establishing its position in the space. The review is a way of defining the restaurant: of making it more or less visible, for instance, or of deciding whether it is a fish or a vegetarian restaurant. Writing a review means giving a particular existence to the restaurant. As a consequence of its rankings and reviews, the restaurant will occupy a particular position in the TripAdvisor space – in a way that is not unlike the changing of its position on a street. If we want to give such a definition of the restaurant – we could say: if we want to grasp its very essence – we must consider numerous factors, including its location (its address in the physical world), the name of its owner, and the dishes it serves, but also its position on TripAdvisor, its visibility on Google, and the collection of comments about it that can be found on online platforms. From an ontological point of view, editorialization contributes to the production of the restaurant because it is a part of its reality. In this sense we editorialize the world itself and not only the information about it. This consideration leads us to a discussion of the *ontological* nature of editorialization.

The Ontological Nature of Editorialization

Let us consider again the opposition between the representational paradigm and the performative paradigm. According to the representational paradigm, we have reality on one hand and discourse on the other: editorialization could be interpreted as a discourse on reality and

---

97   Gottlob Frege, 'Sense and Reference', *The Philosophical Review* 57, no. 3 (1948): 209-230.

therefore as a form of imitation or mimesis. This paradigm has been fundamentally important in the history of Western thought, from Plato all the way to contemporary aesthetics studies. But in digital space reality is a hybridization of connected and non-connected objects. In this sense, reality tends to identify with what Luciano Floridi calls the 'infosphere', as we have seen in the second chapter.[98]

The development of the internet of things is proof of this fusion of reality and the infosphere. Hybridization emerges between the platform and the book in the warehouse. From a technical perspective we cannot properly say that the uniform identifier of an object (URI, for 'uniform resource identifier') is a representation of that object. Indeed, the identifier has an operational power over the object, so that in a sense it becomes the object itself (the URI of Paris is not a representation of the city of Paris; it is the city itself). It is easy to demonstrate this thesis using the example of the distribution system: to order a book on Amazon and to receive it at home hardly requires any human action, and in the future even less than now. Each product has a unique identifier that can be handled on the network, and such an operation directly affects the product itself. I click on a book on Amazon; a robot will search for this book in a warehouse and deposit it on a drone that will deliver it to my address. In other words, there is hybridization between the platform and the book in the warehouse. There is thus no difference between the object of the book and its URI. It is important to underline that a URI does not refer to an object as a common name: the URI is not a generic identifier for a set of objects (like the word 'book') or a set of identical objects (the same book, available in different copies). It refers – or at least it can refer – to a particular object. In other words, a URI does not refer to 'a book' but to a particular book; it does not refer to 'a copy of *The 4th Revolution* by Luciano Floridi', but to a particular copy, to the object itself. There is thus no difference between the object of the book and its URI.

We can take this example further. What is written about a particular object – a comment about a book posted on Amazon, for example – directly affects the object-book because the object-book shares its space with the comments, it is the space of information, the space of the URI (and therefore the object itself), of the comment and the algorithm that handles the procurement and delivery.

It is therefore no longer appropriate to separate the discourse on reality from reality itself: the two are completely hybridized. Once again, editorialization structures our actual space: it is a form of architectural organizing of the spatial positions of things and the relationships between them.

For these reasons, it is also impossible to consider digital space from a purely aesthetic point of view: the paradigm of digital space is an operational paradigm. We *do* things in digital space; we do not simply *look* at them. The critique that Alexander Galloway[99] directs at the work of Lev Manovich[100] is based on this principle. In *The Language of New Media*, Manovich

---

98   Floridi, *The 4th Revolution*.
99   Alexander R. Galloway, *The Interface Effect*, Cambridge, UK, Malden, Mass.: Polity, 2012.
100   Lev Manovich, *The Language of New Media*, Cambridge, Mass.: MIT Press, 2002.

applies the paradigm of audiovisual media to interpret digital space. Digital environments, he insists, must be understood as the space of screens and displays because they are something we look at. Galloway, however, points out that interfaces are not regulated by this structure of looking but rather by a structure of action. Cinema is about aesthetics; digital technology is about action and therefore about ethics.

Let us consider some additional examples. If we look at the editorialization process of a city like Paris, for instance, we see that it would include all the digital maps of Paris (Google maps, Mappy, Openstreetmap); it would also include the trip reviews written by travelers on travel platforms such as Expedia and TripAdvisor, data on Wikipedia or Dbpedia, miscellaneous images, as well as institutional websites (the website of the City of Paris, the websites of its countless museums). When one walks in the city, one is located in an area that is produced by all these practices. To be in Paris is to be in a space in which walls, buildings, and streets coexist with Google maps, information on restaurants, museum opening hours, and an endless variety of other narratives about the city – we can think for instance about all the literature and cinema and art about Paris that contributes in producing what Paris actually is. The city is formed by the aggregate of all these elements and editorialization is the architectural act which allows the production and the organization of this aggregate – and thus the creation of the actual Paris.

The same phenomenon can be seen when looking at Facebook profiles. The Facebook algorithm takes into account the data produced by different profiles and does not consider there to be a difference between a profile and a person. A profile is a person, and as such may be the target of an advertisement or an element of a statistic – a count, for instance, of how many people like an event or how many people have studied at the University of Montreal.

Editorialization, we can therefore conclude, is a way of producing reality and not a way of representing it. This conclusion suggests a problem: if we abandon the representational paradigm, it becomes impossible to distinguish between real and fake or between truth and fiction. The logical definition of truth (Tarsky) is based on the idea of a correspondence between the signifier and the signified. According to Tarsky's definition, 'A' is true if and only if A. For example: the sentence 'it is raining' is true if and only if it is actually raining. But this means that in order to be able to speak about truth, we must have a signifier (the sentence 'it is raining') and a signified (the actual world where it is raining). In the performative paradigm, this distinction is no longer pertinent. Which means that questions about the truth or the authenticity of editorialization are misplaced. We will analyze this problem in the next chapter.

The Multiple Nature of Editorialization

The performative paradigm determines the multiple nature of editorialization: if every act of editorialization produces a reality, then reality must be multiple because there are multiple acts of editorialization. This is a consequence of the very definition of editorialization as a way of organizing the space. As said, editorialization is an architecture of being: it has ontological power. Editorialization is not a way of creating and organizing content and information, it is a way of organizing the world. There is thus a shift from an epistemological to an ontological paradigm. Multiplicity is easy to accept from an epistemological point of view: there is an object which is unique – it has only one essence but many ways of knowing it. This is different when we leave behind the epistemological point of view, as we do with editorialization, which produces not different ways of knowing but different essences. This raises an ontological problem: how can we define the essence of reality if there are many essences?The advantage of the representational paradigm is that it is based on the idea of a unique reality that can be represented in different ways. According to this paradigm one can judge the value of a single representation by analyzing its resemblance to the original. Tarsky's idea of truth is actually an expression of this comparison: we have the reality on the one hand, and the representation on the other, and we can check if the latter is faithful to the former. One could say that the essence of a thing is grasped by the right representation, the one that represents the thing itself most faithfully is the true one.

Abandoning the representational paradigm means confronting many different realities and not having the possibility of choosing between them. This is why editorialization produces a layered reality, a reality that is composed of several different and quite autonomous layers. And this is why the classical ontological approach is not useful for an analysis of digital space: digital space is multiple – originally multiple, one could say – and ontology seeks for an original unity. The ontological approach must be replaced by a meta-ontological approach, which means a theory that accepts an original multiplicity, the multi-essential character of reality.

Let us look at some examples to illustrate this point. A Facebook profile could be considered – according to the representational paradigm – as the representation of the user of whom the profile is the profile. This means that we have on the one hand a 'real' person, the user, and on the other a representation of this person, the profile. We could compare these two objects in order to understand whether the profile is 'true' or 'false', and whether it is faithful to the 'original' object. The idea beyond this paradigm is that the person has a unique essence and the profile tries to grasp this essence. The image of the profile should thus be as close as possible to the person. The aesthetics of the Venetian Vedutismo tradition is a perfect example of this idea: a painting is only as good as it is close to reality, and the goal of a good painter is to push the resemblance to its apex.[101]

But if we understand the online profile not as a form of representation, but rather as a kind of production of identity, we see that there can be many different identities for the same person: a Facebook profile, a Twitter profile, a blog profile, a profile defined on a platform like Amazon or by a research engine, and, of course, the person as a human being, the clothes they wear, etc. All these different profiles create a dynamic conjuncture of circumstances that constitute identity. The person as a human being is only one of many threads. The identity of Marcello Vitali-Rosati is created by my actions, what people think of me, my online profiles, the data collected on me by various platforms and algorithms, the narratives people produce about me on the web or in the university, the comments my students make about me, and so

---

101   For an analysis of representational paradigm and its crisis see Servanne Monjour, 'La littérature à l'ère photographique: mutations, novations et enjeux (de l'argentique au numérique)', PhD Thesis, Université de Montréal, 2015. Monjour proposes the notion of 'anamorphosis' to explain that there is not a privileged model to represent reality: all the representations are distortions.

on. There is no 'original' object in all these. 'Reality' is the superimposition and the dynamic overlapping of these multiple conjunctures. And it is actually possible – or even probable – that these conjunctures are not coherent: the one can contradict the other. For instance, Marcello Vitali-Rosati can at the same time be a very good professor on the platform Ratemyprofessor. com and a very bad one according to the comments made about him on the Facebook page of the student association, a very good one in one semester and a very bad one in another. Clearly, the representational paradigm does not work here: there is not an 'original' and a representation. Instead, all the acts that produce reality are performative and they are all original.

What does this leave us with, then? What is *me*? What is the essence? As we've already seen, there is no single essence but rather *multiple* essences. If ontology is the science of the essence, then meta-ontology is the ontology of multiple essences.[102]

The Collective Nature of Editorialization

Editorialization is always a collective process.[103] This point is also related to the processual nature of editorialization: the process is open and ongoing, it is not possible to draw a border around it. There is no single person or predetermined group of persons who participate in the editorialization: the actor or actors of any editorialization are always part of an open collectivity. This collective dimension is also the main difference between editorialization and content curation. Moreover, without collective action, editorialization is not possible: the action of an individual – even if the individual happens to be a huge enterprise like Google – can never produce an editorialization.

Let us look more closely at the example of Google. One could argue that Google produces a particular structure of content without taking into account the reactions of users. This model could thus be interpreted as Google-centered: there is only one actor who decides how contents are organized; and this actor is the enterprise that conceives and writes the algorithms. But this argument does not hold for three main reasons. First of all, if no one used Google, the algorithm would produce no editorialization. Google can structure content only because people use it. A search engine that is not used has no power to structure content because its structure would remain abstract; it would simply be dead writing, almost inexistent because no one would see it. The power of Google is determined by the fact that there are huge numbers of people using it, and this means that the hierarchy it proposes becomes the actual shape of online content. A page is visible because Google indexes it and because people use Google to find web pages. Second, the algorithm is not static: it evolves according to practices and

---

102 I have spoken about meta-ontology in my books *Corps et virtuel* and *Riflessione e trascendenza: itinerari a partire da Levinas*, Pisa: ETS, 2003. Also see Marcello Vitali-Rosati, 'Voir l'invisible: Gygès et la pornographie Facebook', *Sens-Public*, June 2012, http://sens-public.org/spip.php?article912.

103 This aspect has been underlined by Louise Merzeau, 'Éditorialisation collaborative d'un événement', in *Communication & Organisation* 43, 1 (2014): 105-122. The collective aspect of editorialization is also analyzed by Roberto Gac in his theory of intertext, see for example Roberto Gac, 'Bakhtine, le roman et l'intertexte', *Sens public*, 15 December 2012, http://www.sens-public.org/article.php3?id_article=1007. My work has been deeply influenced by many discussions I have had with Roberto Gac on this topic.

uses. Google must adapt the algorithm to the ways that it is used; if the company were not able to do so, its algorithm would quickly become obsolete. This is why the recording of users' behaviors is crucial for Google: it has to study what people do in order to answer to their needs and even anticipate them. What people do directly affects the algorithm. Third, the algorithm is based on certain cultural values that are pre-determined by collective negotiation. As Dominique Cardon has shown,[104] PageRank is based on the idea of the citation index, which was developed within the academic community: without the collective interactions of this community, these values would simply not exist.

The creation of a profile on Facebook is another example that illustrates how editorialization is never an individual process and always implies a collectivity. When creating a profile on Facebook, a user could be led to believe that they are the only actor in this creation: I can define myself as I want. This idea was well-illustrated in the 90s with the famous sketch of the dog sitting in front of a computer and saying, 'on the internet nobody knows you are a dog'. The idea was that we are completely free to construct our identities however we like. Virtual identity appeared as the realization of the dream of auto-determination: to have the power to re-invent oneself in a completely autonomous way.[105] The problem, in fact, seemed to be an excess of auto-determination: on the internet individuals can pretend to be who they are not.

This dream of auto-determination is clearly false. There are a lot of different factors determining how we produce our profiles: the affordances of the platform, its influence on user behavior, and the practices of other users. We have already talked about the ways in which the technical characteristics of a platform influence our behaviors. It is obvious that Facebook, for example, determines the way I create my profile; the platform is normative because it asks very precise things of me. It is the platform that decides what I can say about myself and how, what is important and what is not, and even, through suggesting a particular rhythm of writing and deciding on which walls my statuses will appear, how often I write and to whom. These aspects are predetermined by the platform. Besides this determination by the platform there is also a set of collective practices and uses that are crucial to the production of my profile: if I am the picture that I choose and the status that I write, I am also the number of friends that I have, the comments that my friends leave on my wall, the pictures of me that other users post and that are tagged, and even the re-use of these pictures in other platforms or contexts.

Once again, we can underline a deep difference between editorialization and the curation of content. If I curate my profile, I am the master of the process, it is about choosing the way we present and structure content. The editorialization of a profile is a set of collective interactions that determines who or what I am: what people know about me and what idea of me they have after looking at my profile.

When trying to grasp the concept of editorialization, it is important to understand a crucial

---

104 Cardon, 'Dans l'esprit du PageRank'.

105 My book *Égarements: amour, mort et identités numériques*, Paris: Hermann, 2014, http://vitalirosati. com/liseuse/spip.php?rubrique3, treats this topic and in particular the relationship between auto-determination and hetero-determination of identity.

problem: the fact that every editorialization is collective does not mean that every editorialization produces something that can be considered as 'common'. In the Google and Facebook examples, the collective aspect clearly does not imply that at the end of the editorialization process we get something common: the data, information, and content that are produced are the property of a private company, and this company decides how these data are produced and for what purpose they are used after their production. In some cases of editorialization, like Wikipedia, we get the feeling that something common is produced, even though it is difficult to look at the platform separately; the visibility and the efficiency of Wikipedia depends largely on the way Google indexes and references it. Therefore a question that we may address is how digital space can be made a public space. In order to answer this question, let us look more closely at the structures of authority that are revealed by the concept of editorialization.

Editorialization and Authority

If editorialization is what structures digital space, and if the structure of a space is the basis of authority – as we showed in the previous chapters – then authority in digital space is created by editorialization. Following this logic, we see that authority in digital space must be processual, performative, multiple, non-representational, and collective. To gain a more precise understanding of what authority is in the digital age, we will examine each of these characteristics in turn.

It should first be emphasized that digital space is hybrid in nature. Digital space is not a self-contained space that is separated from a hypothetical non-digital one. Digital space is our actual space, a space where connected and non-connected objects are merged. This means that there is no separation between digital and non-digital forms of authority, and that digital space is characterized by a hybridization of pre-digital forms of authority and digital ones. Many forms of institutionalized and stabilized authorities that existed before the advent of digital technologies are still operating in digital space, and they co-exist with forms of authority that are native to the digital age.

This point was underlined by Saskia Sassen with reference to the notion of 'capabilities' in her book *Territory, Authority, Rights: From Medieval to Global Assemblages*.[106] Capabilities are characteristics of a specific historical moment that, when organized in a different way, become the basis of the next historical moment. Sassen uses this concept to show that historical changes should not be interpreted as epistemological ruptures but rather as the reorganization of pre-existing cultural principles. In the shift from a medieval feudal order to the order of the nation state, certain medieval capabilities, like the notion of divine authority surfaced in altered form in the political culture: the possibility of a national sovereign, for instance, was guaranteed by the idea of divine authority. In the same way, digital space should be considered as a new political order in which older forms of authority have been reorganized and have taken on new meanings.

---

106 Saskia Sassen, *Territory, Authority, Rights: From Medieval to Global Assemblages*, Princeton, N.J.: Princeton University Press, 2008.

Processual Authorities

One characteristic of this re-organization is that digital authority privileges a dynamic and ongoing process over the crystallized static object. Let us consider again the example of an academic paper. More than most pieces of writing, the academic paper demands an association with the traditional notion of the author. It is an organized, planned action that is signed, and is destined to remain the same through time. Someone takes responsibility for its content, even (and especially) after it has been produced. The signature, the name associated with the content, is the function granting its permanence across time. And yet, when analyzing the conditions of the existence of this content, one rapidly realizes that the signer cannot be considered as the author in the same way as was the case with the printed journal. The authority that makes this specific content reliable is not the author, since the author is a static authority and so can grant legitimacy only if the paper is also static. The editor and the publisher are in the same situation: they also can be an authority only if the paper can be understood in a defined and stable sense. However, as we saw in the previous pages, in the digital space a paper cannot be considered an independent and coherent whole anymore. It is impossible to decide when the process of its production begins and ends, and it is even more difficult to determine in any exhaustive way who is involved in its creation and circulation.

To illustrate this point one needs only to think about the different ways an article is presented. It can be found on a website, using a browser. There, it is not a static page but a code closely connected to a series of other pages and contents. What matters on the page is not only the content but its multiple dynamic relationships with other pages. It is impossible to determine where the content produced by the writer ends and where other content begins. New reading practices support this thesis: one moves from one article to another, from one page to another page, from one piece of research to another, and very rarely does one stop to consider who has produced the content.[107] The signature of the author is, in effect, erased, and the path itself emerges in its place, along with the elements on the page that allow us to walk on the path: links, tags, an address bar or search bar. It is interesting to note that the most common answers to the question 'Where did you find this information?' is 'On the internet' or 'On Google'.

What has become important, then, is not the unity of a text produced by one person – and legitimated by her or him, or by an editor – but the collection of dynamic relationships that this content maintains with other content. And these relationships, which are part of an open process, determine the existence of a piece of content. It is the ensemble of relationships and links that make the content accessible and visible, and thus bring it into existence. Completely independent content would be inaccessible, invisible, actually non-existing.

One cannot therefore consider an article as an independent and static unit, and so the person signing it (or the group that first edited it) should not be considered the authority. The unit is constituted rather by the relationships that make content accessible. But these relationships are not determined by the person who signs an article and are only partially determined by

---

107 Stern, Guédon, and Jensen, 'Crystals of Knowledge Production', p. 1.

the editors and the publisher. Writing and reading actions are merged together in a general editorialization process. Authority becomes a question of the layout of the connections that constitute the space of the web. These connections can derive from the actions of a person reading and moving from one page to the next, or from a series of devices put in place on the web to create relationships, from simple links to algorithms of search engines or commercial platforms like Amazon. In this sense, the answer 'I found this information on Google' is not that naïve because Google is one of the authorities legitimating the content.

Because the process stays open, however, the authority cannot legitimate an object: it has to legitimate a process. This processual authority is clearly not in complete opposition to static authority: the name of the author, along with the names of the editors and the publisher – and their authorities – are all part of the process. Google's algorithm is only one of the processual evaluations and legitimations of the paper, although it has a crucial authoritative function, as we will see in the next chapter.

Another example that illustrates the processual nature of digital authority is Wikipedia. It should first be noted that Wikipedia embodies a hybridized form of authority. As many scholars have pointed out,[108] the dream of an encyclopedic space in which everyone is on the same level does not really come true. O'Neil speaks of 'cyberchiefs' to show how on Wikipedia there is a complex structure hierarchizing different kinds of users. Wikipedia has a very complex bureaucratic architecture that differentiates simple users from administrators and even experts. This means that some pre-digital forms of authority – in this case the authority of the author – endure in digital space. At the same time, it is important to underline that the principles of an article's legitimation on Wikipedia are processual. First of all, the underlying idea of Wikipedia is to maintain a level quality by adhering to certain formal rules. Wikipedia's five pillars are clearly an attempt to define a processual form of authority rather than a static one. On Wikipedia, a piece of content is deemed reliable not because an expert has written it but because it has been produced respecting some very formal norms that strive to regulate the process. As Leitch points out,[109] this attempt has many paradoxes, and some forms of pre-digital authority necessarily infuse this processual authority, but the initial goals and principles of Wikipedia are nonetheless deserving of further analysis. They are:

- First pillar: Wikipedia is an encyclopedia. It combines many features of general and specialized encyclopedias, almanacs, and gazetteers. [...]
- Second pillar: Wikipedia is written from a neutral point of view. [...]
- Third pillar: Wikipedia is free content that anyone can use, edit, and distribute. Since all editors freely license their work to the public, no editor owns an article and any contributions can and will be mercilessly edited and redistributed. Respect copyright laws, and never plagiarize from sources. [...]
- Fourth pillar: Editors should treat each other with respect and civility. Respect your fellow

---

108 See for example Thomas Leitch, *Wikipedia U: Knowledge, Authority, and Liberal Education in the Digital Age*, Baltimore: The Johns Hopkins University Press, 2014; Mathieu O'Neil, *Cyberchiefs: Autonomy and Authority in Online Tribes*, London, New York: Pluto Press, 2009.

109 Leitch, *Wikipedia U*, p. 38.

Wikipedians, even when you disagree. Apply Wikipedia etiquette, and don't engage in personal attacks. Seek consensus, avoid edit wars, and never disrupt Wikipedia to illustrate a point. Act in good faith, and assume good faith on the part of others. Be open and welcoming to newcomers. If a conflict arises, discuss it calmly on the nearest talk pages, follow dispute resolution, and remember that there are 5,013,630 articles on the English Wikipedia to work on and discuss.

• Fifth pillar: Wikipedia has no firm rules: Wikipedia has policies and guidelines, but they are not carved in stone; their content and interpretation can evolve over time. Their principles and spirit matter more than their literal wording, and sometimes improving Wikipedia requires making an exception. Be bold but not reckless in updating articles, and do not agonize about making mistakes. Every past version of a page is saved, so any mistakes can be easily corrected.[110]

These principles are processual: they say something about how the process of production should be structured, but they say nothing – or almost nothing – about a static validation or valuation of content. The only validation is the possibility of structuring the process. The first principle is a definition of the format of the content: Wikipedia content must be encyclopedic. This provides a format rule, which has the effect of conditioning and structuring the production process. The second is the most famous – and controversial – principle. As Leitch points out, it is impossible to determine what a neutral point of view is (because a neutral point of view is itself a point of view), and so the claim to represent a neutral point of view is not really a neutral position. But at the same time, the idea behind this principle is to provide a formal rule that makes possible an evaluation of the validity of the production process. This principle is often associated with the rule of always citing a source: anyone, regardless of their level of expertise, can evaluate the process of production of an article because they can just check to see if the article cites its sources or not. The third and fourth principles underline other process evaluation policies: the respect of copyright and the need for civility when resolving conflicts. The fifth principle most clearly aims to establish a processual form of authority: there are no firm rules, the production of knowledge is a process, everything can be changed, and all mistakes can be corrected. The reliability and the quality of Wikipedia rest on the fact that it is both a regulated and an open process.[111] As O'Neil states, 'Wikipedia depends on a radical redefinition of expertise, which is no longer embodied in a person but in a process: the aggregation of many points of view'.[112]

Beside these principles there is the technical element: the platform itself. MediaWiki, the Content Management System (CMS) used by Wikipedia, is designed to structure and organize the process of writing in a specific way. The CMS plays an important role in the production of authority: determining the way users interact, content is linked, and algorithms verify that principles are respected, and even to the extent that the ergonomics

---

110 See https://en.wikipedia.org/wiki/Wikipedia:Five_pillars.

111 Dominique Cardon, 'Surveiller sans punir: La gouvernance de Wikipédia', in Lionel Barbe, Louise Merzeau, and Valérie Schafer (eds) *Wikipédia, objet scientifique non identifié*, Sciences humaines et sociales, Nanterre: Presses universitaires de Paris Ouest, 2015, http://books.openedition.org/pupo/4092, pp. 15-39.

112 O'Neil, *Cyberchiefs*, p. 149.

and graphics function as formal constraints that structure and influence the production process. This is what Cardon calls 'the recursive dependency of practices and rules'.[113] This point brings us to another characteristic of digital authority: its performative quality.

Performative Authorities

Editorialization, as we established earlier, is performative in the sense that it produces its own norms; it does not represent things but rather produces them. Such a self-producing quality also characterizes digital authority. This is made quite clear when we consider the deep relationship between activity and authority, which is something that has been demonstrated by many scholars.[114] The more active a user is, the more authority the user attains; acting, in digital space, means producing authority. We see this in the way that a simple user becomes an administrator: certainly on Wikipedia, but also in many other discussion forums or platforms only very active users seem to be administrators. Authority is about activity, irrespective of the kind or quality of the activity. A user is reliable because they are present.

This principle applies to users' authority, but it is even more applicable to the authority of platforms: visibility depends on activity and visibility produces authority. The more a platform is active, the more it is visible and the more it is considered reliable. Google and its classification philosophy based on the citation index is a very good example of this principle. The idea underlying PageRank is that the more a piece of content is cited, the more authority it gains. But this implies a performative effect in the production of authority: a page is cited because it is visible and Google places it on the top of the results list. This implies that being visible determines an increase in visibility, and an increase in visibility signifies an increase of authority. Authority in this sense tends to be concentrated in digital space.

Non-representational Authorities

An important consequence of this element of performativity is that authority cannot be understood using a truth-based model. Authority does not guarantee that content – whether a sentence, an image, a video, web page, or any other fragment of information – corresponds to reality: authority is what creates reality. This is related to the ontological nature of editorialization. This characteristic is actually not specific to digital space. If we return to Arendt's definition of authority, we see that authority does not stem from the fact that we can verify its information. Authority is something we trust without any rational cause. In other words, something is true because an authority says that it is true. On the other hand, we cannot say that an authority is an authority because it states the truth. But the fact that the authority *produces* the truth means that it is impossible to verify what the authority says. Verification itself cannot be a criterion of authority.

---

113 Cardon, 'Surveiller sans punir, p. 19. For this structure of validation of information, see also Juliette De Maeyer and Avery E. Holton, 'Why Linking Matters: A Metajournalistic Discourse Analysis', *Journalism: Theory, Practice & Criticism* 17:6 (August 2016): 776-94, https://doi.org/10.1177/1464884915579330.

114 For example Leitch, *Wikipedia U*, and Dominique Cardon, *La démocratie internet*.

It is therefore impossible to question authority on the basis of verification of fact. This is an important point that will be at the center of the next chapter: authority must be questioned – or at least questionable – if we do not want it to be transformed in absolute power. The risk of being transformed in absolute power is something that is intrinsic to authority, but it is a risk that is perhaps more visible in digital space because of the ontological nature of editorialization.

How can we question, for example, the fact that the top-ranked result for a piece of research on Google is the most pertinent result? The higher a page is on the PageRank ranking, the more visible it is. And the more visible it is, the more it is viewed and cited. In the set of values decided by the algorithm, the most often-cited page is the most pertinent. The sentence 'The page which is the first Google result is the more pertinent' is true because of the fact that this page is the first Google result: Google authority produces the truth of the sentence, or more precisely it transforms it in a tautology. In order to question this structure we need another legitimating system, which means another authority that we can trust more than Google's. In that instance, however, we would simply have two opposing truths: the one of Google and the other one.

Another example to illustrate this point is the Wikipedia principle of 'Verifiability':[115] reliability of information is not based on its truth (because no one can verify this truth) but on the fact that sources can be cited in support of the information. Verifiability is thus not the possibility of comparing the information with the facts, but just the possibility of comparing the information with other information.[116] This idea echoes what we said about meta-ontology: there is no essence of things but rather multiple essences – as many as there are discourses that can circulate in digital space – because there is no longer a separation between objects, facts, and discourses. This leads us to the question of the relationship between the multiple nature of editorialization and authority.

Multiple Authorities

Editorialization is always multiple. This multiplicity determines, in particular, the crisis of the concept of the 'original'. In print-dominated culture, a pillar of authority was the production and conservation of documents. The fact that a state owns the right to produce and conserve a birth certificate, for example, gives the state the authority to grant identity to its citizens. We trust the state when it tells us that a person was born on this day and has this name because we know – even if we do not verify – that there is a document proving these facts. The original document is the proof and owning the original is a kind of authority. The possibility of verification exists, even if the proof is produced by the same authority that afterwards owns it. One could ask to see the original – or to have an authenticated copy, which means a copy that the authority confirms 'conforms to the original'. In digital space, though, there is no more original, because of the multiplicity of each piece of information, data, or document. The document is an entry in a database, but it is not possible to distinguish the entry on a particular database from the same entry in another database. A birth certificate can be on multiple databases simultaneously. It can be owned by multiple institutions and by multiple states, by universities

---

115   See, https://en.wikipedia.org/wiki/Wikipedia:Verifiability.
116   Cardon, 'Surveiller sans punir, pp. 27-28.

where the person has studied, and by past and present employers. These entries can be exactly the same or they can be different; any number of variations is conceivable.

It is thus no longer possible to use the concept of the original as a proof of truth. Authority can make something reliable only through a validation process. Instead of basing the reliability of information on the existence of an original, it is now necessary to grant this reliability with the active recognition of information. For example, if an employer needs proof of an employee's date of birth, instead of asking the employee to provide the original birth certificate, the authority could create a validation process that allows the employer to compare the information the employee has provided with the information that is available in the authority's database. This is exactly what happens in semantic web practices, where an 'authority' is a Uniform Resource Identifier that identifies an object in a unique way on a specific database.[117]

For example, if one wants to know the list of books published by me, and be sure that the author is me and not somebody else – for instance, a homonym – one can refer to the Library of Congress and learn that the URI corresponding to me is http://lccn.loc.gov/n2009013771. This link is a tool that enables the validation of my identity in the Library of Congress database. But the Library of Congress is only one of many authorities. One could decide, for instance, that, because I have written most of my books in French, it is better to trust the Bibliothèque Nationale de France: the URI for Marcello Vitali-Rosati is http://catalogue.bnf.fr/ark:/12148/cb15021926p/PUBLIC, another 'authority'. In one database I am the author of three books, in the other the author of five.

Digital space is thus characterized by the coexistence of many authorities and these authorities can be different and often contradictory. This multiplicity also determines that in digital space pre-digital authorities coexist with authorities that are native to digital space. For example, Google is an authority that determines and measures the pertinence of content and an academic journal is an authority in much the same way. In digital space it is true that a page is pertinent because it is the first on a Google research list and that another is more pertinent because it is on the site of a well-known academic journal. In practice we accept that many authorities can coexist – even those that are very different from one another – and that we can trust all of them, though perhaps in different ways. We can trust TripAdvisor, Wikipedia, Google, and at the same time the institutional site of a university, an academic journal, or the website of the government – authorities that are all very different and that are based on very different models.

Collective Authorities

The collective nature of editorialization is probably its most problematic aspect. Digital space is clearly a matter of collective dynamics: this is the main characteristic of a network. But

---

117 Another good example of this kind of validation process is blockchain technology: a list of records which are maintained in a distributed way. The authority of a record is not based on its original but, on the contrary, on the fact that there are many copies of the same records and a protocol that allows to share and compare them.

what kind of collectivity is involved in editorialization processes? Digital space is produced by a continuous interaction between people, machines, algorithms, and platforms. This idea is what determines our definition of editorialization as the set of interactions of individual and collective actions within a particular digital environment. Authorities emerge from these interactions. The fact that PageRank has became an authority depends on the algorithm (its values, its rules) and on the platform (its graphics, its ergonomics, its interface), which in turn interact with multiple practices: people using Google, web masters adapting their sites for SEO, enterprises buying data, and so on. Authority grows based on these interactions. In this sense, authorities are not organized in a clear and stable hierarchy.

In the space of the nation state, there is certainly a collective aspect to authority. But this aspect is weaker because of a clear and stable hierarchy that organizes the relationships between authorities. An Aristotle specialist has the authority to decide whether a paper on Aristotle is good or not: their authority is granted by their degree, which is granted by a university, which is accredited by the state (in the case of a public university). The system is hierarchically organized: if we do not trust the state, it is difficult to trust the university, and if we do not trust the university, we will not trust the degree, and if we do not trust the degree, we will probably not recognize the scholar's authority. Obviously, this model is not quite so monolithic. We can turn again to Saskia Sassen's notion of capability to understand that in the pre-digital academic model there was something that, organized in a different way, could produce the digital model. This is apparent, for example, in the concept of 'peer' and the system of the citation index according to which the value of a paper should not depend on the credentials of its author. In digital space, though, it becomes impossible to identify any kind of hierarchy because only the result of the dynamic interactions counts, and this result is never stable.

At the same time, the fact that authorities are not organized in a hierarchical way does not mean that some are not stronger than others. There are stronger and weaker authorities – because of their influence field, the degree of trust they inspire, and the number of people over whom they have authority. But the relationships between these authorities are not structured as they were in pre-digital society: there is no hierarchical relationship between Amazon's authority and Google's authority or Facebook's.

In digital space, authorities can appear suddenly (and also suddenly disappear). They are always the result of the recursive dynamic between collective practices and digital structure. But what exactly does 'collective' mean?

I am using this term in a very formal sense, which means that I am not giving it any political signification: 'collective' is simply whatever involves more than one person. In this sense, everything in digital space is collective. But does this mean that everything is common? Does it mean, in other words, that some collectivity is the master of digital space and the primary actor of its production? Clearly, this is far from true.

The strongest authorities in digital space are powerful enterprises for whom non-hierarchized organization offers the possibility of cultivating an ultra-capitalist model of liquid power, as

Morozov has shown in his books.[118] Often the collective aspect is only a way of exploiting people to enrich a private enterprise. The cases of Uber and Airbnb are very meaningful. The economical model of these platforms is based on their reliability: users know that they can trust them. But this reliability is produced by users themselves, for example through the evaluation system. On Uber and in Airbnb each user is evaluated by the other: a landlord is nice, his apartment is more or less beautiful or well situated, a driver is on time, a passenger is polite...: everything is evaluated in such ways. People make these evaluations – without being paid. Every person involved is in some way controlled by others (drivers are evaluated by passengers, passengers are evaluated by drivers, hosts by guests, and guests by hosts). The enterprise exploits the mutual control of people in order to produce capital. This is what some scholars describe as digital labor.[119] Instead of producing commons, collectivities produce capital. Is it possible to transform these structures? What are the collective interactions that can produce commons? What can be a common authority? These are the questions that will be addressed in the final chapter of this book.

---

118 Evgeny Morozov, *The Net Delusion* and *To Save Everything, Click Here: The Folly of Technological Solutionism*, New York: PublicAffairs, 2013.
119 Dominique Cardon and Antonio A. Casilli, *Qu'est-ce que le digital labor?* Bry-sur-Marne: INA, 2015; Christian Fuchs and Sebastian Sevignani, 'What Is Digital Labour? What Is Digital Work? What's Their Difference? And Why Do These Questions Matter for Understanding Social Media?', *tripleC: Communication, Capitalism & Critique* 11, no. 2 (2013): 237-93.

5. WRITING THE PUBLIC SPACE

Criticizing Authority

Authority exists in digital space. There are dynamics within digital space that produce trust in a way that corresponds with Arendt's definition of authority as something one trusts without a rational reason and without being forced. The existence of authority in digital space is not a problem *per se*, in my opinion. The libertarian utopia of a space without authority is a naïve and simplistic interpretation of the complex structure of digital space. Moreover, this naïve utopia should not be confused with the anarchist ideal of a space that is free from centralized power. As we have already shown, authority can generate power, but power and authority are not the same thing. In Arendt's analysis, power and authority can even be in opposition to one another because authority produces trust without needing the use of power. We trust certain aspects of the digital realm because digital space is a structured space and we recognize this structure, even without completely understanding it. As stated earlier, the structure of a space is what produces its authority. And it is quite possible for an authority to exist without a transcendent power structure.

There are however some problematic aspects of digital authority that need to be addressed. The first is the difficulty of interpreting it critically: as discussed in the first chapter of this book, an authority must be questioned. An authority is always related to a particular space and so understanding the space makes it possible to relativize the validity of a specific authority. Understanding the space can mean the first step in limiting the extent of the authority. This possibility is crucial because an unquestionable authority easily turns into a violent power. Trust in an authority should therefore always be accompanied by an ability and willingness to criticize and question it. The problem for digital authorities is that the relatively new structures of the space make it difficult to understand them, and understanding is necessary in order to critique them. Moreover, the performative and non-representational nature of digital authorities means that we have fewer tools to question them: the truth paradigm, based on the possibility of verification, in useless. Also, the dynamic nature of digital authorities and their non-hierarchized structure present a fundamental problem in studying them and having a critical consciousness of them. Theory develops itself more slowly than practice evolves, and so by the time we are able to identify a structure, the structure has ceased to exist or at least has changed enough for another theory to be necessary.

The second problematic aspect is the difficulty of understanding how digital authorities relate to both the public and the private sphere. If authority depends on a space, it is crucial to know how this space is produced and whether it can be considered a public space or not.[120] In other words: are digital authorities private or public? A question that in itself raises problems, because the border between private and public is blurred in digital space. Everything seems to be public, but it is very difficult to determine whether this public aspect implies the production of something common.

---

120 My analysis of public space at the time of the digital owes much to my discussions and work
     with Gérard Wormser. See in particular Gérard Wormser, 'Banco !... L'espace public à l'heure du
     numérique', *Sens Public*, 17 December 2010, http://www.sens-public.org/article800.html.

These two problems are the main political issues in digital space; addressing them is the first step towards developing what Geert Lovink calls 'Net criticism'.[121]

Public and Private

We have established that digital space is inclusive: an object can simultaneously belong to two different spatial structures. It can be at the same time be inside and outside, visible and invisible. This implies that, in terms of visibility, the relationship between public and private is blurred. A picture can be private within the particular configuration of the Facebook space – because I can set the privacy level of the picture, granting access only to my friends – and public if one of my friends publishes it on another website. What I considered private is also public.

The distinction between private and public can no longer be based on visibility: we must therefore find some other way to characterize; if indeed it is a distinction. What is public? What is private?

We should first note a paradox in the way the public sphere has been defined: on the one hand, as a space without power; on the other, as the space of power. Habermas pointed out this ambiguity in *The Structural Transformation of the Public Sphere*: 'We call events and occasions "public" when they are open to all', but we call a building a 'public building' when it is owned by the State, and a public building is not open at all, it 'does not even have to be open to public traffic'.[122] Moving from this ambiguity, Habermas shows how, in the eighteenth century, social realms were divided into two opposing parts: the private realm and the realm of public authority. The public sphere, paradoxically, is part of the private realm. In fact, the private realm is on the one hand the realm of commodity exchange, of labor, and of the family's internal space, and on the other the sphere where private people meet for purposes of public interest – for example, discussing arts and letters and culture in general. The bourgeois public sphere is thus, according to Habermas, where private people come together, organizing the space without the constraints of public authorities. An example of this sphere is the French salon.[123]

Another space where private people meet for public purposes is the public square, a large and empty place where people can get together and where their behavior supposedly is not controlled. The Agora in classical Greece was actually imagined as an empty space for this very reason:[124] the authorities had to leave the space empty in order for the public sphere to exist. A lack of structure and authority allows private people to negotiate the structure themselves: they can create something public. At the same time, it is obvious that this lack of any

121 Geert Lovink, *Dark Fiber: Tracking Critical Internet Culture*, Cambridge, Mass.: MIT Press, 2002.
122 Jürgen Habermas, *The Structural Transformation of the Public Sphere: An Inquiry into a Category of Bourgeois Society*, Cambridge, Mass.: MIT Press, 1999, pp. 1-2.
123 Lionel Ruffel criticizes Habermas' notion of public sphere and underlines the very elitist aspect of it. Habermas' public sphere is related only with bourgeois culture and does not represent the majority of people. Ruffel proposes the concept of 'brouhaha' (the noise of crowds) as an alternative to define public space. See Lionel Ruffel, 'The Public Spaces of Contemporary Literature', *Qui Parle: Critical Humanities and Social Sciences* 22:2 (21 March 2014): 101-22.
124 Olivier Mongin, *La condition urbaine: la ville à l'heure de la mondialisation*, Paris: Éditions du Seuil, 2007, p. 78.

structure in the public sphere is a myth: the square is an architectural artifact and the very authorities that should have been kept out of it have defined its architecture and still control it. In this sense, as Steven Flusty shows,[125] public space is not a space of freedom but rather a space of constraints: everything is designed to control and direct people's behaviors. The empty square is itself a tool of control.

Taking into account these contradictions, we can attempt to put forth a preliminary definition of 'public' that works for digital space. First, public is always something that concerns a collective: a public building concerns a collective because public institutions organize the collective; the State – whether it is democratic or not – is the function that organizes a collective and is therefore public; public opinion is public because it is shared by a collective. Public is what concerns a collective in a passive or active mode. The problem with this definition is that it is too broad: almost everything in digital space would be public according to it. The definition is useful to distinguish the private sphere as a sphere of behaviors that do not concern a collective: for example, freedom of religion is based on the eighteenth century idea that individual religious beliefs do not concern the collective and so should be permitted in whatever form. Religion is not a public issue. In digital space, however, everything seems to be collective, as the theory of editorialization states. But does this mean that everything is public? Can we say, for instance, that a Facebook page is public? Or that a proprietary algorithm like PageRank is public?

In order to delimit the sense of the term, we should say that, in digital space, 'public' is what concerns a collective in an active sense – which means that public is what is produced by a collective. We can broadly define 'collective' as a group of people that is not necessary organized, more precisely public is something that is owned by a collective and that is accessible to the collective. In this sense, we can link the concept of public to the notion of 'common'.[126] But this notion must also be clarified. In the sense that it is used for the phrase 'common lands', for instance, common refers to something being owned by somebody – often a state – but a collective has easement of it, the right to use it. The problem with this definition of 'common' is that, in digital space, almost everybody seems to have easement of almost everything. We can use whatever we want even if we rarely own what we use. Can we say, for example, that all the Google environment is a common because everybody has easement of it? For the notion to have a meaning in digital space, common must imply collective ownership, or at least an absence of private ownership. From these considerations we can propose a first definition of digital public space. A digital space is public when:

• It is produced by and for a collective. As with the Greek Agora, digital space is public when the shape and the structure of it are not predetermined by a power that precedes the collective. This means that the very structures of the space, its way of creating relationships between objects, are negotiated in a collective way and not imposed by an individual, a

---

125 Steven Flusty, *Building Paranoia: The Proliferation of Interdictory Space and the Erosion of Spatial Justice*, West Hollywood: Los Angeles Forum for Architecture and Urban Design, 1994.

126 For a study on the notion of commons, see Elinor Ostrom, *Governing the Commons: The Evolution of Institutions for Collective Action*, Cambridge, United Kingdom: Cambridge University Press, 2015.

group, a company, or a state. At the same time, the space is produced for a collective, which means that this collective is self-conscious and thinks about itself as a coherent unit. As with the Greek Agora, digital space is public when the shape and the structure of it are not predetermined by a power that precedes the collective.

• It is owned by a collective. It is difficult to establish the exact meaning of ownership in digital space, but we can say that a collective ownership exists when there is no private ownership.

• It is accessible to a collective. In order for it to be considered public, the collective must always have access to digital space. Every access restriction, at any level, implies that the space is not public.

It is tempting to say that a private space is the opposite of a public space, but it would be more accurate to understand these two realms on a scale of continuity: a space is not *either* public or private; a space is more or less public and more or less private. The two extremes represent poles in a continuum, but neither purely public nor purely private spaces exist in reality.

Everything is Private

This definition of 'public' is actually very restrictive. If an inclusive definition of public as something that involves a collective is too broad to be applied to digital space (because everything in digital space involves a collective and could be considered public), this more exclusive definition risks the opposite effect: nothing seems to be truly public in digital space. This is approximately the main thesis of Morozov's work,[127] whose theoretical essays follow a long tradition of analyzing the progressive privatization of public spaces. Habermas, for example, has described how the bourgeois public sphere as it was developed during the eighteenth century began to decline as society and the state became increasingly merged, a process that was completed by the development of mass media. According to Habermas, bourgeois society was organized in such a way that everything concerning business was part of the private realm. The public sphere was possible because business was considered of no interest for public matters. The private realm and the public realm were clearly separated, and the public sphere belonged to the private realm. Beginning in the nineteenth century, however, 'powers of society themselves assumed functions of public authority',[128] which meant that private and public realms began to overlap and squash what lay between them: the public sphere began to disappear. A double phenomenon can be observed here: the realm of business and work becomes of public interest and begins to influence politics; as a reaction, states become more interventionist in the realm of business and work. This implies a 'socialization of the state' and a parallel 'statelization of society'. The economical stakes in the cultural industry are a part of this phenomenon: during the eighteenth century arts and letters were clearly separated from the realm of the state, they were a part of the private realm but distinguishable from commodity and family, being part of the public sphere. Now, mass media do not belong to the public sphere anymore because it involves private economical stakes.

---

127 Morozov, *The Net Delusion* and *To Save Everything, Click Here.*
128 Habermas, *The Structural Transformation of the Public Sphere*, p. 142.

This overlapping of private interests and the public sphere is described by Saskia Sassen in reference to the increasing privatization of cities: 'Cities are the spaces where those without power get to make a history and a culture, thereby making their powerlessness complex. If the current large-scale buying continues, we will lose this type of making that has given our cities their cosmopolitanism.'[129] The empty space, the space where a lack of authority allows powerless people to build their own public space, becomes a corporation's property. The public sphere ceases to exist.

Morozov's analysis of the role of Silicon Valley corporations starts from the same stance: what should be public on the web is actually private. The domains of public interest are owned by big companies, and the services that should be granted by public authorities are instead organized and provided by private corporations. Morozov underlines the fact that Silicon Valley corporations propose services for democracy using what he calls the 'solutionism': all social problems can be solved with technological tools, which are produced by Silicon Valley corporations or start-ups. Important political issues are reduced to organizational problems and are no longer considered public. An individualistic point of view underpins this ideology: everything is managed according to how it can make the lives of individuals easier and more comfortable. The problem is thus twofold: private corporations own most of digital space and they impose their ideologies on the whole social space, leaving no room for a public sphere. Private corporations decide what the structure of digital space is and what values it holds.

One could again deduce that nothing can really be public in digital space. Collectives are reduced to an aggregation of individuals who have neither a critical perspective on what is of public interest nor a consciousness about their even being a collective.

Following our first definition of 'public', we might say that next to nothing in digital space is made by and for a collective because the spatial structures of digital space are prede-termined by corporations, which provide individuals with solutions for private problems. Moreover, these spaces are owned by private companies and are not always accessible to the collective.

Let us consider some examples. Google's search engine, for instance, is the result of certain collective interactions. Without a group of people using Google and adapting their practices to its principles, the search engine would cease to exist. But can we consider what Google produces as public? The spatial structure of the Google results list is in a sense co-produced: it is created through the interaction of individuals and collective practices. But this collective has no self-consciousness. Google provides individuals with a service; the service is not made for a collective. The company decides on the shape and structure of the space for a disparate set of individuals who are never considered as a coherent group forming a collective. And the structure of this space is not really negotiated with a collective: it is in the hands of Google,

---

129 Saskia Sassen, 'Who Owns our Cities – And why this Urban Takeover Should Concern Us all', *The Guardian*, 24 November 2015, http://www.theguardian.com/cities/2015/nov/24/who-owns-our-cities-and-why-this-urban-takeover-should-concern-us-all.

who can adapt it to the needs of the target group but who always thinks about this group precisely as a target and never as an active subject.

While it is obvious that Google is not made for a collective, it is more difficult to decide on questions of ownership and accessibility. Google's Terms of Service policy states: 'You retain ownership of any intellectual property rights that you hold in that content. In short, what belongs to you stays yours.'[130] They are not talking about the search engine here but rather about all Google services that presuppose the uploading of information (such as Google Drive, Google Calendar, or Gmail). In such cases, the user retains ownership of the information but gives Google the authorization to use all of it. In fact, Google has the easement of all this information. In the case of the search engine, Google does not only search for information on the web (web crawling) but also caches web pages and stores them on its servers. In a proper, legal sense, Google is not the owner of this information. But in a more practical sense, is this still true? Let's consider what happens when I produce a piece of information about myself and put it on my website. This information is then indexed by Google and stored in its caches. Even if I delete the information on my website, it is still on Google's servers and remains available for other users. Am I still the owner of this information? In legal terms, yes, but practices show that this legal idea is not effective anymore. The same thing could be said about accessibility. The Google ideology is to make everything accessible to everyone. Collectively, though, we can access only some of the data. Other data – a huge portion (including personal data, such as the history of user queries) – is owned by Google and can be sold to other companies for advertising purposes. We don't have access to this, let alone that we can sell it ourselves.

The same considerations are true for other big Silicon Valley corporations, especially those that make up the acronym GAFAM (Google, Apple, Facebook, Amazon, Microsoft). Though these companies have different policies, they all have the same effect on public space: they squash it by reducing every potential collective to a collection of individuals who are targets of their corporate actions, or even products. For them, collectives are at most involved in a passive way: they observe the behavior and actions of individuals to improve algorithms or obtain data about them, but the collective is never seen as an active, coherent entity. Even the idea of considering the collective as a statistical trend has lost its appeal; it turns out to be more worthwhile to target users individually. Pre-digital branding strategies were based on identifying groups that might be interested in particular products or brands. In digital space data about each individual is collected and it is no longer important to identify groups: each user has become a separate target. The customization of the homepage of Amazon is an example of this: the homepage is different for each user, according to their profile.

Digital Labor

A seemingly paradoxical consequence of this broad privatization of digital space is that every-thing online seems to be free. This appears as a paradox because we are used to thinking that we pay for private services and do not pay for public services. Our relationship with online material functions differently, however: online services seem free but are meant to

---

130 See https://www.google.com/policies/terms/.

compel users to produce value for the companies providing the services. This phenomenon has been described as digital labor.[131] Users have the idea that they are provided with a particular service for free – for instance, they have access to reviews of all the restaurants in the world on TripAdvisor – but in reading and adding to such material, they are actually working for the companies providing the services without being paid:

> Online activity creates content, social networks and relations, location data, browsing data, data about likes and preferences, etc. This online activity is fun and work at the same time – play labour. Play labour (playbour) creates a data commodity that is sold to advertising clients as a commodity.[132]

This means that users are actually producing capital for the companies. Fuchs and Sevignani underline that this activity must be described as labor and not as work because the means of production are owned by the companies and not by the collective. Work should be understood as a necessary activity that produces use-value, in contrast to labor, which only produces value and is based on some form of exploitation. What we do when we use online services is produce value for the companies providing these services; we are thus exploited by these companies.

The cases of Uber and Airbnb are instructive. Both companies provide a service using the solutionism described by Morozov: you need a taxi, and there is no taxi company available in the area, or hasn't got enough taxis or is too expensive. But now you can use the service of Uber, which allows you to get in touch with a driver who wants to drive you. If you want to find a place to sleep and hotels are too expansive or there are none of them, Airbnb lets you find a private owner who wants to rent out their apartment. On the surface, these services appear to be improving exchanges within a collective: communicating with other people is becoming easier and easier, and now almost everything seems to be done without having to go through a private company (like the taxi company or the hotel). But while these services leave us with the impression that private interest is no longer involved, this is not really the case at all. First of all, there is actually a company, Airbnb and Uber, even if we do not realize that we are paying them. Secondly, the functioning of these platforms is based on the principle that users produce value for these companies: by proposing our offers, writing a review, by rating our experience, we are providing for free the information that ultimately becomes the product that the company sells. The existence of Uber and Airbnb depends on the fact that they own information – about drivers and passengers or about owners and hosts. Uber can tell you whether a driver is reliable or whether a passenger is kind; Airbnb can give to you the same information about apartments, owners, and hosts. But users produce this information, which is afterwards owned by the company. The same thing can be said about TripAdvisor, for instance, or Amazon. Everything a user does online constitutes a kind of labor that ultimately produces value for a company.

The only way to solve this problem, according to Fuchs and Sevignani, is to ensure 'that means of communication as means of production such as YouTube become communalized so that

---

131 Cardon and Casilli, *Qu'est-ce que le digital labor?*; Fuchs and Sevignani, 'What Is Digital Labour?'.
132 Fuchs and Sevignani, 'What Is Digital Labour?', p. 237.

the Internet turns from a corporate Internet in to a commons-based Internet nourished by the creative work of use'.[133] This brings us again to the question of the relationship between public and private. Earlier we said that, in order to be public, digital space must be produced by a collective. All the 'public' services provided by internet corporations are based on a space that has been produced by corporations. This is what Fuchs and Sevignani mean when they speak about 'means of communication as means of production' in Marxist terms. The space of YouTube, the space where users' actions take place, is designed and structured by YouTube. This space is not public, and the actions that take place within it are exploited by the corporation that has designed and structured it, namely, Google or better, Alphabet. In other words, digital labor is possible because the space where actions take place is not public. For this reason, it is crucial to identify the border between private and public space in the digital realm.

The Border Between Public and Private

Understanding whether a space has been designed and structured by a collective or by a private interest – like a corporation – is not easy. The main problem is that as users we often have the feeling of being in a public space when in fact we are in a private one: this is the trick of digital labor. Digital labor and the exploitation that comes with it are possible only because users are oblivious to their own exploitation: they think they are using a free service, that they are clients, when in reality they are working for a corporation, providing it with unpaid labor.

A form of violent authority is based on the same structure. The fact that digital space is structured by corporations implies that these corporations have become the authorities within this space. At the same time, the role of these corporations is hidden by the fact that the space seems to be public. As a result, we are left with the impression that there is no authority involved at all. Authority has become something quite different from the thing described by Arendt. Rather than being something we trust in a particular space, it is what Kojeve describes as 'the possibility that an agent has of acting on others without these others reacting against him despite [their] being capable of [it]'.[134] We do what an authority asks us to do not because we trust it but because we are not aware that we're being asked to do something.

In other words, understanding what is public in digital space means understanding the extent of our freedom as users and, ultimately (because digital space is the space we live in), as human beings. Every action is more or less determined by a particular context and this context can be interpreted as a space. Now, if this space is public, it means that the action is determined following a common negotiation. If the space is not public, it means that another actor, with its own distinct purposes and interests, is determining the action.

The structure of a space determines an action in the sense that structure always carries certain values. The structure of a space is the context of the action, and so it shapes and gives meaning to it. And as the analysis of editorialization made clear, this space is an overlapping of technol-

133 Fuchs and Sevignani, 'What Is Digital Labour?', p. 287.
134 Alexandre Kojève, *The Notion of Authority: A Brief Presentation*, London: Verso, 2014, p. 8.

ogy, culture, and practices, and the three aspects can only be separated in a purely theoretical way. This is why it is difficult to distinguish a public space from a non-public one. In order to be public, a space must be produced for and by a collective. In the case of Google, for example, the technological aspect is certainly determined by the corporation, but the other two aspects are co-determined by a collective. Google's algorithm is founded on a culturally inscribed idea – the meritocratic classification of content – that is neither specific to the corporation nor owned by it. And the development of the algorithm is based upon user practices.

In order to be public, a space must be produced for and by a collective. The idea of ownership, too, is very difficult to apply to digital space, where objects are essentially multiple. This is why I propose that the public and the private be placed on a continuum rather than in a discrete opposition to one another. Every space should be understood as being more or less public. And the degree to which the space is public can be assessed by observing in what degree a collective actively participates in the negotiation of the space itself.

Let us use this publicity scale to consider two examples: Facebook and Wikipedia. One could say that Facebook is completely private and Wikipedia is completely public, and that only Wikipedia produces something that could be considered common. Instead of putting these two platforms in opposition, though, we could analyze them along a continuous line. We could then draw the following conclusions.

Firstly, the spaces of Facebook and Wikipedia are both produced by and for a collective. In the case of Facebook, though, the collective has an active role only in the production of the cultural and practical aspects of the space. Facebook is conditioned by a particular cultural context that pre-dates the platform and that is produced by a collective. Facebook is also influenced and shaped by users' practices: what users do with the platform pushes the platform to change. Even the very mission of Facebook has been determined by user practices: the initial idea was to rank Harvard students according to their attractiveness: 'The website used photos compiled from the online facebooks of nine Houses [of Harvard University], placing two next to each other at a time and asking users to choose the "hotter" person'.[135] While it was built as a campus tool, the goal and the essence of the platform changed when many students registered and then forwarded the site to other campuses. Following the habits of its users it now became a photo sharing service for campuses. So what people actually did was different from the initial idea of the project, users' behaviors changed the goal of the platform and contributed to transform it into a worldwide social network. But the technological aspect of Facebook is not negotiated collectively: it is in the hands of the corporation. And even with the first two aspects, the cultural and the practical, the corporation must approve every change. This means that the degree to which the space can be considered public is quite limited. In the case of Wikipedia, the collective can negotiate the space from cultural, practical, and technological points of view because the CMS on which Wikipedia is based is an open source CMS (MediaWiki) and everybody can see how it works (they can see the code) and contribute to its development. Further, all the rules of Wikipedia are explicitly

135 Katherine A. Kaplan, 'Facemash Creator Survives Ad Board', *The Harvard Crimson*, 19 November 2003, http://www.thecrimson.com/article/2003/11/19/facemash-creator-survives-ad-board-the/.

negotiable (as the fifth pillar says: 'Wikipedia has no firm rules'). Wikipedia's level of publicity is obviously higher than Facebook's. At the same time, there are many spatial structures that are not negotiable on Wikipedia either. An example is the lower layer of protocols on which every online platform is based: this is the communication protocol of the internet; it carries values and at the same time influences and shapes our actions.[136] Moreover, even if the technological structure is theoretically open, only a limited number of people is actually capable of understanding how it works, and an even smaller number is able to change it. Moreover, in terms of the possibility of changing the rules, as we have already shown, some very strong power situations exist within the community and there is actually no real equality between users – with most active users on Wikipedia being cyber-chiefs of a sort.[137] Wikipedia is thus 'more' public than Facebook, but it would be inaccurate to say that Facebook is not public and that Wikipedia is public.

Secondly, the spaces of both Facebook and Wikipedia are to a certain extent owned by a collective. On the one hand, it is true that Facebook's space is owned by Facebook. But, on the other hand, it is also true that data produced by users remains to some extent the property of these users. The second principle of Facebook (Ownership and Control of Information) states: 'People should own their information. They should have the freedom to share it with anyone they want and take it with them anywhere they want, including removing it from the Facebook Service'.[138] Even if one could state that this principle is not actually respected, its existence shows that the nature of the platform is ambiguous. The Wikipedia platform is based on a GNU Free Documentation License, which is intended to leave the ownership in the hands of a community: it is thus far more public than Facebook. At the same time, the infrastructure of Wikipedia is owned by a private foundation (The Wikimedia Foundation) whose principles cannot be negotiated in a completely collective way. Again, while Wikipedia is clearly more public than Facebook, it is inaccurate to say that Facebook is not public and Wikipedia is.

Thirdly, the spaces of both Facebook and Wikipedia are partially accessible to a collective. The accessibility of Facebook is decided primarily by the company itself, but it is to some extent also determined by users. With Wikipedia accessibility is almost total – one can access everything and modify almost everything. Again, though, for reasons of infrastructure, access is shaped and limited by the very material infrastructure of the internet: in order to access Wikipedia, we must pay an internet provider and use cables that are owned by corporations, typically telecommunications corporations.

Concluding, interpreting 'public' and 'private' as qualities that exist along a continuum makes it impossible to classify digital space and digital practices in Manichean terms. It is not possible, in other words, to separate the good ones from the bad ones, good platforms from bad platforms, good users from bad users, or good practices from bad practices. This more complex vision allows us to identify differences among commercial and privately owned

---

136 Alexander R. Galloway, *Protocol: How Control Exists after Decentralization*, Cambridge, Mass.: MIT Press, 2004.

137 O'Neil, *Cyberchiefs*.

138 See https://www.facebook.com/principles.php.

digital enterprises: for example, the ideology behind Google lends itself to a higher degree of publicity than the one on which Facebook is founded; while accessibility is one of the first pillars of Google's philosophy, this is not the case with Facebook.

The complexity of human action that characterized pre-digital spaces is thus found in digital space as well. There are many different practices and many different interpretations of these practices; there are many stakes involved and many shades of meaning that need to be analyzed in order to arrive at a political understanding of digital space.

The Pessimistic Argument

Let us return to the two main problems that are addressed in this chapter: the difficulty of making a critical interpretation of digital authority and the difficulty of distinguishing private authorities from public authorities. From a very pessimistic point of view we could say that, first, it is impossible to have a critical understanding of digital authority because it is always hidden. The existence of digital labor is proof of the impossibility of identifying authorities in digital space: we work for a company without being aware of it, and we even think that we are receiving a free service. And second, it is impossible to distinguish public authorities from private authorities because the notions of public and private are completely blurred in digital space. In fact, everything is collective, but the meaning of this collective is reduced to a sum of individuals who are nothing more than advertising targets. According to this radical critique, the very structure of digital space implies the impossibility of critical thinking: in digital space, it is impossible to build a public space.

This pessimistic argument has the merit of underlining certain risks. It is true that digital authorities are often hidden and that it is quite difficult to distinguish private entities from public ones. But this argument has a limitation: it considers all the practices and all the actions that take place in digital space as part of a unified and homogeneous whole. What this pessimistic argument does not consider is that digital space – like every other actual space – is a context in which a set of heterogeneous practices and actions unfold and in which many different kinds of actors are implicated. It is crucial, if we want to avoid a generic and superficial interpretation, to take into account this diversity and plurality.

The plurality of practices is at the same time a plurality of behaviors and of technical possibilities. In other words, users can behave – and do behave – in many different ways within the same platform, and these same users, of course, behave on many different platforms. Let us first examine the plurality of behaviors. The pessimistic argument is actually rather paternalistic in the way that it considers users as a homogeneous – and probably not very clever – mass. The thinking behind this argument is that a platform has its rules and coaxes users to do things in order to be able to manage them and obtain data about them; users simply follow along without being aware of what is going on. An example of this pessimistic argument that corresponds to the discourse of mass media is the contention that Facebook coerces users into putting pictures online, or displaying private content, or presenting themselves in a particular way (the way the platform suggests by way of its particular affordances and constraints),[139] ultimately adhering to a predetermined pattern of behavior that benefits Facebook itself. In doing so, users do not realize that they are being directed and exploited by the platform. While it is undeniably true that Facebook has many affordances and constraints – as discussed in the previous chapter with respect to the technological aspects of editorialization – one cannot deduce from this fact that every user behaves in the same way. An attentive study of user behaviors, like the one proposed by Morrison,[140] shows that each user page deserves to be read and analyzed closely. In other words, if one would look at Facebook profiles as a set and analyze them in a statistical way, one could confirm the hypothesis of the pessimistic argument, but if each profile is read closely it can be seen that each user has a unique way of dealing with Facebook's affordances and constraints, and that users often demonstrate sophisticated levels of awareness of the platform's stakes and implications. This awareness can express itself in the ways that they present their status (by using irony, for instance, or by simply not answering the question 'What's on your mind'), or in their profile pictures, or even in their name choices. Although it is Facebook's policy that real names be used, the practice of using pseudonyms is very common. This plurality of behaviors has a huge impact on the policies of the platform and so the platform is continually forced to change itself, in order to adapt itself to actual practices and to accept deviations from standard behaviors. Ultimately, users are not dumb.

It is true that this plurality of practices does not prevent commercial platforms from exploiting users' actions – and the data collected by them. Analyses of behavior are more and more focused on individuals rather than on statistics. Algorithms analyze patterns of behavior by focusing on each user's actions. Even a non-standard practice – which is difficult to interpret from a statistical point of view – can be easily understood from the point of view of an individual analysis. Profiling algorithms enable the collection of a large amount of data about one particular person as a way of identifying that person for commercial purposes. This is why the plurality of practices cannot be the only response to the pessimistic argument. Another response has to do with the fact that commercial platforms are not the only platforms in digital space. They have a central role, certainly, but they do not fully capture the experience of digital space. We have looked at the example of Wikipedia as a space that is more public compared to Facebook. But there are millions of different digital experiences – platforms, websites, applications, and software of all kinds – that are characterized by greater or lesser degrees of publicity.

In the following pages I will propose a deeper analysis of these two responses to the pessimistic argument.

Digital Literacy, Détournements, and Tactical Media

Authority is not, in and of itself, a problem: we need authorities. If we accept Arendt's definition, authority is not only necessary; it is also the condition of freedom. Totalitarian powers, in her view, result from an absence of authority that is then filled with violent power. When there is

---

139 Aimée Morrison, '"What's on Your Mind?": The Coaxing Affordances of Facebook's Status Update', in Julie Rak and Anna Poletti (eds) *Identity Technologies: Producing Online Selves*, Madison, Wisconsin: University of Winsconsin Press, 2013, pp. 112-131.

140 Morrison, '"What's on Your Mind?"'.

nothing we naturally and willingly trust, power forces us to do what it wants with violence. Digital space is full of authorities in Arendt's sense. There is never a need to force anybody: we do everything not only without being forced, but also with the feeling that we can do whatever we like. The notion of digital labor again is proof of this: we work without knowing that we work and without being forced to do it. In a sense, this situation can be understood as an excess of authority that guarantees that no violence will be necessary. But, undeniably, the fact that we are rarely aware of the presence of authority and of its structures has the potential to be a serious problem: it creates the possibility that we will become completely exploitable, so that authorities will be able to coax us into doing whatever they want.

Understanding how digital space is structured and the stakes that are involved is the first step towards resisting the overwhelming power of corporations and being able to produce a public space. Understanding is also the key to contextualizing and limiting the validity of an authority, no matter what kind of authority it is. Again, the pessimistic argument is paternalistic because it considers users as an oblivious mass, an undifferentiated group who do not understand what is going on in the space they inhabit. Certainly, it is true that we are accustomed to interpreting the structures of pre-digital space and so are better equipped to deduce its rules, values, and forms of authority, and that with respect to digital space we are in less familiar territory. Everybody is able to understand that the White House is a place of power, or that the structure of a classroom gives power to the professor: we are familiar with the architecture and we can easily interpret what it means. A big isolated house, with impressive appearances and surrounded by a garden, that is difficult to access and situated in a strategic position in town, tells us that this is an important spot. A very visible stage in a room, with all the chairs disposed in order to look to at the stage, along with the presence of a projector tell us that we should listen to the person on the stage. It is more difficult to understand how and why Google or Facebook or Airbnb have authority.

I think it is important to stress that this is only partially true. As I said earlier, users are not dumb. We normally have an intuitive understanding of the rules of the space we inhabit. We intuitively grasp that Google has authority, and we understand the characteristics of what I described as editorialization. Clearly, though, this understanding could (and should) be deeper and more structured. Digital literacy is perhaps one of the most important issues of our time. And understanding how digital space is made is not only a technical matter or a prerogative of computer specialists: it is the condition of understanding our political situation. Digital space is the space where we live, it is the space where politics unfold: understanding it is therefore necessary for being a free and aware citizen, it is on the same level as studying history or political science.

Understanding digital space makes it possible to identify its authorities, to question them, and sometimes to oppose and resist them. There are many forms of resistance that are based on the idea of short-circuiting the structure of a space and giving it a different meaning and value. This kind of action is what the Situationists used to call 'détournement'. *Détourner* literally means 'to divert' or 'to turn away'. The term is based on the notion of space: the main idea of the Situationists was to give spaces another meaning by doing things within them that were not predicted by the structure of the space itself. An example of détournement is the notion of 'dérives',[141] which refers to a sort of random journey in an organized architectural space. Débord's idea was that by randomly walking in a strongly organized space – like the one of a town – we question its architectural structures, become aware of them, and finally we oppose them.

The same kinds of practices are present in digital space, not only in artistic practices but also in the everyday practices of 'normal' users.[142] Using Facebook to create a literary character, using a pseudonym instead of a real name, using a funny picture to represent ourselves in a 'serious' context, or using a hashtag to make a word a keyword – all these are practices that change the meaning of a particular digital space. And by realizing these actions, users become more aware of the structure of digital space. Using a fake name on Facebook, for example, will often lead to a block from the platform – because its policy includes the idea that names must be real names. If a user is blocked while attempting to use a fake name, they will be aware of a Facebook policy that probably they did not know before. At the same time, these practices have an impact on platforms, which are forced to change or to adapt themselves to such non-standard practices, that are very common in digital space.

Indeed, a key difference between these practices and the Situationist détournement is that they are not limited to artists or to elites. This is why we can make a link between such practices and what Geert Lovink calls 'tactical media'. Tactical media are 'a set of dirty little practices, digital micro-politics if you like. Tactical media inherit the legacy of "alternative" media without the counterculture label and ideological certainty of previous decades'.[143] In other words, tactical media can be everyday practices that try to force and short-circuit the meaning of mainstream platforms, which have become de facto authorities.

Digital literacy combined with tactical media or détournement practices are in my view very strong reactions to the risk underlined by the pessimistic argument. At the same time, these practices are not necessarily 'public'. Although they are often undertaken by politically aware groups, in many cases the practices only reflect the actions of individuals. How can digital literacy or tactical media or practices of détournement produce something public? This is an especially crucial question since private companies, as we have seen, have demonstrated the will and the ability – thanks to algorithms – to recuperate individual behavior for marketing purposes. Therefore, the only effective way to resist and to avoid the dire predictions of the pessimistic argument is to produce something that is genuinely public in the sense that it comes from a collective that is aware of being a collective.

---

141 Guy Debord, 'Introduction to a Critique of Urban Geography', *Les Lèvres Nues* #6 (September 1955), http://www.cddc.vt.edu/sionline/presitu/geography.html.

142 See for example, Sophie Limare, *Surveiller et sourire: les artistes visuels et le regard numérique*, Montréal: Presses de l'Université de Montréal, 2015, and Servanne Monjour, 'Dibutade 2.0: la "femme-auteur" à l'ère du numérique', *Sens public*, 24 September 2015, http://sens-public.org/article1164.html..

143 Lovink, *Dark Fiber*, p. 254.

Free Software

The first possibility for short-circuiting the pessimistic argument is found in the plurality of behaviors and practices. The second is found in the plurality of technologies. Digital technology is not a monolithic entity: there are many different technological entities and each one has its own characteristics, its own values, and its own social and political consequences. The key to understanding this plurality is to avoid reducing the reality of technology to the industry discourse about it. The reality of technology is multiple and complex; the dominant discourse about it is monolithic, oversimplified, and teleological. We are deeply influenced by this discourse and our experience of technology is driven by it. Adhering to the Silicon Valley narrative in a non-critical way actualizes all the risks that the pessimistic argument warns of. A good first step to counter this, then, is to identify some of the characteristics of this discourse. In particular, let us analyze the ideas of progress and simplicity. One of the foundations of corporate communication and advertising is the rhetoric of progress: each product is an improvement of its precedent. A quick analysis of the presentation of any new product will show that the most frequently used key expressions are 'improvement', 'additional features', and various comparative forms like 'faster', 'better', 'higher', and 'simpler'. (We will return to the last one in a moment.) 'Diversity' is never a point. A new product is never simply different, it is always better: this means that technology is presented in a linear development, as if its goals and its purposes were pre-defined and so the only thing to do is to get closer and closer to 'the perfect' technology, the 'best', the 'fastest', the 'highest', the 'simplest'. This is the teleological ideology of industrial discourse: everything tends toward a predetermined end; and the only challenge is to know who (or what brand) will be the first to reach this end. The reason industrial discourse is based on this ideology is really quite trivial: in order to sell new products, a company must explain why the new version is worthy. All marketing is founded on the teleological argument. Progress induces purchase. This ideology of course offers a very distorted view of reality: even a superficial look at the history of technology shows that there is no linearity and no final goal. Many scholars have analyzed the relationship between technological development and social, political, economical, and cultural factors, and have shown that there is no linear progression, but rather a kind of oscillation of a multiplicity of aspects that depend on a range of conditions.[144] Another crucial point is the one about diversity: this ideology does not allow any form of difference. There is only one goal and only one end. It is clear to everyone and no one can question it. Who has decided this final goal, who has established the values behind it, and why this is a worthy goal is not a question that industrial discourse permits us to ask. Obviously, this situation produces a strong and unquestionable authority: based on the principle of this linear structure, there is only one form of reliability – and thus only one authority. The most reliable is the brand that develops fastest, the one that is deemed the most able to reach the final goal first.

---

144   See for example, Carolyn Marvin, *When Old Technologies Were New: Thinking about Electric Communication in the Late Nineteenth Century*, New York, Oxford: Oxford University Press, 1990 and Servanne Monjour, 'La littérature à l'ère photographique: mutations, novations et enjeux (de l'argentique au numérique)', Ph.D. Thesis, Université de Montréal, 2015.

The second keyword of industry discourse deeply linked with the first one: simplicity. Simpler is better. Every product should work out of the box, without the need for instructions, studying, or effort. For this to be possible, though, there is one condition to respect: the goals and the purposes of technology must be unique and clear to everybody. This perfectly captures the solutionism described by Morozov: everyone has the same needs and technology must provide an answer to these needs. The fact that different practices may exist is not taken into account. The fact that many different values could exist at the same time is not considered possible. The simplicity argument is dangerous because it implies a broad movement towards standardization and because it reduces the possibility of critical thinking. Users shall neither know how things work, nor shall they ask themselves what they need: the solution comes before the question.

As said earlier, industrial discourse should not be confused with technological reality. The standardization that it proposes does not correspond with the multiplicity of existent possibilities. It is true that the most widely used technological services are the ones proposed by a small number of multinational corporations (like GAFAM), but it is also true that there are more and more alternatives available that open up the possibility of a critical relationship with digital space. The existence of these alternatives improves our chances of assuming a critical political point of view: choosing what technologies we use is a political act.

A phenomenon worth examining in this context is free software. The notion of free software was first developed by Richard Stallman in 1983, with the GNU project, which aimed to create a completely free operating system and which gave birth to GNU-Linux. Here is the definition of free software given by the Free Software Foundation:

"Free software" means software that respects users' freedom and community. Roughly, it means that the users have the freedom to run, copy, distribute, study, change and improve the software. Thus, "free software" is a matter of liberty, not price. To understand the concept, you should think of "free" as in "free speech," not as in "free beer". We sometimes call it "libre software" to show we do not mean it is gratis.[145]

This definition is important because it makes clear the relationship between software and politics by providing an answer to the initial question of this chapter: How can we make digital space a public space? If we come back to the three conditions for a digital space to be public, we notice that the philosophy of free software actually respects these conditions to a very high degree.

- *It is produced by and for a collective.* The idea of community is the first cited in free software's definition. The community is the group of people working for the development of the software and then using it. Without a deep sense of the community, free software could not exist. And it needs to be a self-aware community. Creating free software means, first of all, negotiating collectively the values, principles, and goals of the software. It is

---

145 See https://www.gnu.org/philosophy/free-sw.html and Richard Stallman, 'Why Open Source Misses the Point of Free Software', https://www.gnu.org/philosophy/open-source-misses-the-point.html.

important to underline the difference between free software and open source. As the Free Software Foundation says: 'Open source is a development methodology; free software is a social movement. For the free software movement, free software is an ethical imperative, essential respect for the users' freedom. By contrast, the philosophy of open source considers issues in terms of how to make software "better" – in a practical sense only.'[146] In other words, the awareness of the collective of itself as a collective, one that has chosen and negotiated its values and its principles, is a characteristic of free software and not necessarily of open source. On the contrary, the open source notion can be used – and is used – to feed the logic of digital labor, which involves exploiting individuals' work to increase corporate profit.[147]

- *It is owned by a collective.* The work on licenses has been one of the more important developments of the free software community. Free software is developed under the GNU General Public License.[148] The main principles of this license are intended to make it impossible to create private ownership. Free software is always in the public domain.
- *It is accessible to a collective.* Accessibility is one of the pillars of the free software movement because its existence is based on it. In order to be developed, free software must be accessible. Everything is thus accessible: the source code and its versions, the discussions about the development, the documentations.

The free software approach enables the creation of a digital public space and makes a critical view on it possible because it allows us to understand the principles and reasons behind its structures.

Open Access

If accessibility and collective ownership are two necessary conditions for a space to be public, it is important to give some consideration to the philosophy of open access. The analysis of editorialization that we proposed earlier suggests that we should treat all forms of the production of public space as a whole: software and technology production should not be separated from knowledge production because both are part of a unique dynamic. Open access of scientific knowledge is crucial: such knowledge was typically a part of the public sphere as defined by Habermas. The privatization of this knowledge in digital space is one of the main problems to be solved if we want to avoid the risks underlined by the pessimistic argument. Open access has many implications, including issues of copyright politics and notions of fair use,[149] economic and institutional issues,[150] as well as more broad philosophical and political issues. I will focus here on the philosophical and political implications of open access.

---

146 See https://www.gnu.org/philosophy/open-source-misses-the-point.html.
147 Evgeny Morozov, 'The Meme Hustler', *The Baffler*, April 2103, http://thebaffler.com/salvos/the-meme-hustler.
148 See https://www.gnu.org/licenses/gpl.html.
149 See for example, Michael Geist (ed.) *The Copyright Pentalogy: How the Supreme Court of Canada Shook the Foundations of Canadian Copyright Law*, Ottawa: University of Ottawa Press, 2013.
150 See for example, Peter Suber, *Open Access*, Cambridge, Mass.: MIT Press, 2012, and 'Good Practices for University Open Access Policies – Harvard Open Access Project', 2016, http://cyber.law.harvard.edu/hoap/Good_practices_for_university_open-access_policies.

In 2012, 47% of scientific papers – both in natural and medical sciences and in social and human sciences – were published by five major companies: Reed-Elsevier (24.1%), Springer (11.9%), Wiley-Blackwell (11.3%), American Chemical Society (3.4%), and Taylor & Francis (2.9%).[151] This situation deeply diminishes the possibility of producing a public space: content which is produced with public funding becomes private. In fact, scientific content is actually often produced within public institutions. So, content that is initially produced by and for a collective (which pays for its production but also negotiates and determines the principles and the structure of the production), has been given to a private entity that owns it and that determines its accessibility. In term of authority, this signals a movement from public authorities – universities and scientific communities – to private ones. The structure of digital space is partially the cause of this aberration – as Larivière shows the situation is getting worse with the beginning of digital dissemination – but the ambiguity of digital space implies that its structures also give the means to overturn the situation. As discussed in the previous chapter, digital space is characterized by a paradoxical tendency to both produce multiple and fragmented authorities and to concentrate authority in specific places. This contradictory tendency may be driven by our behaviors in the sense that practices determine how authority is concentrated or fragmented.

In concrete terms, this means that scientific communities, if they are aware of the problem and are conscious of their status as a collective, can easily bring about a shift in this tendency. A recent study of institutional policies demonstrates such effectiveness of an open access mandate for institutions.[152]

These considerations about the impact of user behavior, free software, and open access are strong arguments against a certain form of fatalism that characterizes the pessimistic argument. In other words, digital space does not *per se* imply the impossibility of producing a public space. The possibility of a robust public space remains and it is our responsibility to realize it. As with every space, digital space is a frame that influences actions and presents certain possibilities, but it does not determine them.

---

151 Vincent Larivière, Stefanie Haustein, and Philippe Mongeon, 'The Oligopoly of Academic Publishers in the Digital Era', *PLoS ONE* 10, no. 6 (2015): e0127502, doi:10.1371/journal.pone.0127502.

152 Philippe Vincent-Lamarre, Jade Boivin, Yassine Gargouri, Vincent Larivière, and Stevan Harnad. 'Estimating Open Access Mandate Effectiveness: The MELIBEA Score', in *Journal of the Association for Information Science and Technology (JASIST)* 67 (2016), http://eprints.soton.ac.uk/370203/.

CONCLUSIONS

We can now briefly summarize the results of this book and suggest further investigations.

Digital space is the space in which we live. It is the set of relationships between a hybridization of connected and not connected objects. Digital space is material, and the adjective 'digital' should be considered less as a reference to technology than as signifier of period: there is modern space, there is contemporary space, and then there is digital space. Digital space is the space of today's societies.

A space is the frame and the context of actions. In that sense a space always carries values: understanding the structure of a space means understanding the conditions of the possibility of actions and their signification.

The structure of digital space is produced by what we call editorialization, which is the dynamic interaction of individual and collective actions within a particular digital environment.

Authority is something we trust without being forced and without being rationally convinced.

The structure of a space determines the forms of authority that are found in it. Editorialization therefore determines the forms of authority in digital space. The fact that digital space is different from other well-known forms of space leads to the feeling that there is a lack of authority within it. But this is far from true. Studying editorialization allows us to recognize and understand the characteristics of digital authorities.

The principal risk of digital space is that it is susceptible to a concentration of authority and this concentration can be difficult to identify. This can lead to the emergence of powerful central authorities whose power resides partially in the fact that we are not even aware of them.

The main challenge of digital space is to understand how it can be made public. Producing a public space means producing the possibility of public authorities that can be questioned.

Our behaviors and our technological choices influence the degree in which digital space is public. It is our responsibility to make digital space a public space.

These conclusions have a central philosophical implication: space is the structure that permits the production of meaning. This might seem strange if we remember that a harsh critique of space has been used to characterize the twentieth century – with its structure of objectivization that reduces everything to an objective, static, and given unity. Bergson's critique of space as a structure of juxtaposition was probably the first of these critiques:[153] time, he suggested, is a structure that allows differences, while space is the scientific notion

---

153 Henri Bergson, *Essai sur les données immédiates de la conscience*, Paris: P.U.F., 1948.

that prevents all possibility of difference. Time allows the possibility of subjectivity, and space reduces each subject to an object.

Digital space reveals that the materiality of space is not necessarily static. Space is dynamic – even if it is material – and it is negotiated through the interactions of individuals and collective practices. Moreover, space is multiple, which implies that space can produce multiple meanings.

This opens the door to a philosophical problem, which we presented briefly in the third chapter: space is a notion that grants the possibility of objectivity and unity. The fact that space is multiple and dynamic creates a crucial ontological problem, though. It implies the necessity of a multi-essential reality.

This multiplicity can be a problem because it can lead to a radically constructivist approach to reality, according to which we produce reality as we wish without there being a given structure that determines our interpretations. The problem with the constructivist idea is that it allows the strongest holders of power to construct reality to their advantage. This was underlined in our analysis of the concentration of authority in digital space. Multiplicity may engender the production of public meaning, but it may also lead to the privatization of meaning. The problem, then, is to discover a way of allowing multiplicity without descending into a radical constructivism. This was a central problem for philosophy during the last century. Digital space renews this problem and poses it in more urgent and practical terms.

I have suggested that meta-ontology is an approach that allows us to understand the multiplicity of reality without losing the coherence of our interpretations. In this sense, developing a meta-ontological approach is probably the more crucial challenge for philosophy.

BIBLIOGRAPHY

'2nd Page Rankings: You're the #1 Loser | Gravitate Online', *Gravitate Online*, 12 April 2011, http://gravitateonline.com/2011/04/12/2nd-place-1st-place-loser-seriously/.

Aarseth, Espen J. *Cybertext: Perspectives on Ergodic Literature*, Baltimore: Johns Hopkins University Press, 1997.

Agostini-Marchese, Enrico. 'Les structures spatiales de l'éditorialisation: Terre et mer de Carl Schmitt et l'espace numérique', *Sens Public*, 10 March 2017, http://sens-public.org/article1238.html?lang=fr.

Arendt, Hannah. *Between Past and Future: Eight Exercises in Political Thought*, New York: Penguin Books, 2006.

Austin, John Langshaw, and James Opie Urmson. *How to Do Things with Words: The William James Lectures Delivered at Harvard University in 1955*, Cambridge, Mass: Harvard University Press, 2009.

Bachimont, Bruno. 'Nouvelles tendances applicatives: de l'indexation à l'éditorialisation', in *L'indexation multimédia*, Paris: Hermès, 2007, http://cours.ebsi.umontreal.ca/sci6116/Ressources_files/BachimontFormatHerme%CC%80s.pdf.

Beaude, Boris. *Internet, changer l'espace, changer la société: les logiques contemporaines de synchorisation*, FYP éditions, 2012, http://www.beaude.net/icecs/.

Benjamin, Walter, and Michael William Jennings, Brigid Doherty, Thomas Y. Levin, and E.F.N. Jephcott (eds). *The Work of Art in the Age of its Technological Reproducibility, and Other Writings on Media*, Cambridge, Mass.: Belknap Press of Harvard University Press, 2008.

Bergson, Henri. *Essai sur les données immédiates de la conscience*, Paris: P.U.F., 1948.

Bourrelly, Laurent. 'Google Vanity Ring', *Observatoire Google*, 18 November 2007, http://google-observatoire.blogspot.it/2007/11/google-vanity-ring.html.

Brin, Sergey and Lawrence Page. 'The Anatomy of a Large-Scale Hypertextual Web Search Engine', *Computer Networks and ISDN Systems* 30, no. 1-7 (April 1998): 107-117, doi:10.1016/S0169-7552(98)00110-X.

Bush, Vannevar. 'As We May Think', *Atlantic Magazine*, July 1945, http://www.theatlantic.com/magazine/archive/1945/07/as-we-may-think/303881/.

Butler, Judith. *Excitable Speech: A Politics of the Performative*, New York: Routledge, 1997.

Cardon, Dominique. 'Dans l'esprit du PageRank', *Réseaux*, vol. 177, nr. 1 (2013): 63-95, http://www.cairn.info/resume.php?ID_ARTICLE=RES_177_0063.

_____. *La démocratie internet: promesses et limites*, Paris: Seuil, 2010.

_____. 'Surveiller sans punir: La gouvernance de Wikipédia', in Lionel Barbe, Louise Merzeau, and Valérie Schafer (eds) *Wikipédia, objet scientifique non identifié*, Sciences humaines et sociales, Nanterre: Presses universitaires de Paris Ouest, 2015, http://books.openedition.org/pupo/4092.

Cardon, Dominique, and Antonio A Casilli. *Qu'est-ce que le digital labor?* Bry-sur-Marne: INA, 2015.

Cascone, Kim. 'The Aesthetics of Failure: "Post-Digital" Tendencies in Contemporary Computer Music', *Computer Music Journal* 24:4 (2000): 12-18.

Dahlgren, Peter. *The Political Web: Media, Participation and Alternative Democracy*, London: Palgrave Macmillan, 2013.

Debord, Guy. 'Introduction to a Critique of Urban Geography', *Les Lèvres Nues* #6 (September 1955), http://www.cddc.vt.edu/sionline/presitu/geography.html.

De Maeyer, Juliette and Avery E. Holton. 'Why Linking Matters: A Metajournalistic Discourse Analysis', *Journalism: Theory, Practice & Criticism* 17:6 (August 2016): 776-94, https://doi.org/10.1177/1464884915579330.

'Disputatio pro Declaratione Virtutis Indulgentiarum – Wikisource', https://la.wikisource.org/wiki/Disputatio_pro_declaratione_virtutis_indulgentiarum.

Doueihi, Milad. *Digital Cultures*. Cambridge, Mass.: Harvard University Press, 2011.

_____. *Pour un humanisme numérique*, Paris: Seuil, 2011.

Douglas, J. Yellowlees. *The End of Books or Books without End?: Reading Interactive Narratives*, Ann Arbor, Wantage: University of Michigan Press, 1999.

Eco, Umberto. *Lector in fabula*, Paris: Librairie générale française, 1985.

Eisenstein, Elizabeth L. *The Printing Press as an Agent of Change*, Cambridge: Cambridge University Press, 1980.

Farrell, Henry. 'The Consequences of the Internet for Politics', *Annual Review of Political Science* 15, no. 1 (2012): 35-52, doi:10.1146/annurev-polisci-030810-110815.

Farrell, Henry, and Daniel W. Drezner. 'The Power and Politics of Blogs', *Public Choice* 134, no. 1-2 (2007): 15-30, doi:10.1007/s11127-007-9198-1.

Ferraris, Maurizio. *Âme et iPad*, Parcours Numériques, Montréal: PUM, 2014, http://www.parcoursnumeriques-pum.ca/ameetipad.

Floridi, Luciano. *The 4th Revolution: How the Infosphere Is Reshaping Human Reality*, New York, Oxford: Oxford University Press, 2014.

Flusty, Steven. *Building Paranoia: The Proliferation of Interdictory Space and the Erosion of Spatial Justice*, West Hollywood: Los Angeles Forum for Architecture and Urban Design, 1994.

Foucault, Michel. 'Des Espaces Autres', *Architecture, Mouvement, Continuité*, no. 5 (1984): 46-49.

Frege, Gottlob. 'Sense and Reference', *The Philosophical Review* 57, no. 3 (1948): 209-230.

Fuchs, Christian, and Sebastian Sevignani. 'What Is Digital Labour? What Is Digital Work? What's Their Difference? And Why Do These Questions Matter for Understanding Social Media?', *tripleC: Communication, Capitalism & Critique* 11, no. 2 (2013): 237-93.

Gac, Roberto. 'Bakhtine, le roman et l'intertexte', *Sens public*, 15 December 2012, http://www.sens-public.org/article.php3?id_article=1007.

_____. 'Éditorialisation et littérature: du roman à l'intertexte', 18 March 2016, *Sens public*, http://www.sens-public.org/article1185.html?lang=fr.

Galloway, Alexander R. *Protocol: How Control Exists after Decentralization*, Cambridge, Mass.: MIT Press, 2004.

_____. *The Interface Effect*, Cambridge, UK, Malden, Mass.: Polity, 2012.

Geist, Michael (ed.). *The Copyright Pentalogy: How the Supreme Court of Canada Shook the Foundations of Canadian Copyright Law*, Ottawa: University of Ottawa Press, 2013.

Genette, Gérard. *Seuils*, Paris: Points Seuil, 2002.

Gervais, Bertrand. 'Naviguer entre le texte et l'écran: penser la lecture à l'ère de l'hyper-textualité. in J. M Salaün et C Vandendrioe (eds.) *Les défis de la publication sur le web: hypercultures, cybertextes et méta-éditions*. Lyon: Presses de l'Enssib, http:/www.enssib.fr/sites/www/files/documents/presses-enssib/ebooks/defis-e-book.pdf.

Gibson, William. *Neuromancer*, New York: Ace Books, 1984.

'Good Practices for University Open Access Policies – Harvard Open Access Project', 2016, http://cyber.law.harvard.edu/hoap/Good_practices_for_university_open-access_policies.

Gualtieri, Lisa Neal, and Janey Pratt. 'Dr. Google', *Magazine of the Tufts University Medical and Sackler Alumni Association* 68, no. 1 (2009): 14-18.

Guyot, Brigitte. *Sciences de l'information et activité professionnelle*, vol. 38, C.N.R.S. Editions, 2004, http://www.cairn.info/resume.php?ID_ARTICLE=HERM_038_0038.

Habermas, Jürgen. *The Structural Transformation of the Public Sphere: An Inquiry into a Category of Bourgeois Society*, Cambridge, Mass.: MIT Press, 1999.

Harkless, Gresham. 'Importance of Showing up on the First Page of Google – The Unique Side of Entrepreneurship', *The Unique Side of Entrepreneurship*, 18 July 2012, http://progreshion.ceopress.com/2012/07/18/importance-of-showing-up-on-the-first-page-of-google/.

Kaplan, Katherine A. 'Facemash Creator Survives Ad Board', *The Harvard Crimson*, 19 November 2003, http://www.thecrimson.com/article/2003/11/19/facemash-creator-survives-ad-board-the/.

Kojève, Alexandre. *The Notion of Authority: A Brief Presentation*, London: Verso, 2014.

Kittler, Friedrich. *Optical Media*. Cambridge, UK, Malden, Mass.: Polity, 2009.

Landow, George P. *Hypertext: The Convergence of Contemporary Critical Theory and Technology*, Baltimore: Johns Hopkins University Press, 1992.

Larivière, Vincent, Stefanie Haustein, and Philippe Mongeon. 'The Oligopoly of Academic Publishers in the Digital Era', *PLoS ONE* 10, no. 6 (2015): e0127502, doi:10.1371/journal.pone.0127502.

Lefebvre, Henri. *La production de l'espace*. Paris: Éditions Anthropos, 1974.

Leitch, Thomas. *Wikipedia U: Knowledge, Authority, and Liberal Education in the Digital Age*, Baltimore: The Johns Hopkins University Press, 2014.

Lessig, Lawrence. *Code: And Other Laws of Cyberspace, Version 2.0*, New York: Basic Books, 2006.

Lévy, Pierre. *Qu'est-ce que le virtuel?*, Paris: Éd. la Découverte, 1995.

Limare, Sophie. *Surveiller et sourire: les artistes visuels et le regard numérique*, Montréal: Presses de l'Université de Montréal, 2015.

Lovink, Geert. *Dark Fiber: Tracking Critical Internet Culture*, Cambridge, Mass.: MIT Press, 2002.

_____. *My First Recession: Critical Internet Culture in Transition,* Rotterdam: V2_NAi Publishers, 2003.

Luther, Martin. 'Disputation of Doctor Martin Luther on the Power and Efficacy of Indulgences', *Wikisource,* https://en.wikisource.org/wiki/Disputation_of_Doctor_Martin_Luther_on_the_Power_and_Efficacy_of_Indulgences.

Lyon, David (ed.). *Surveillance as Social Sorting: Privacy, Risk, and Digital Discrimination,* London, New York: Routledge, 2003.

MacKinnon, Rebecca. *Consent of the Networked: The Worldwide Struggle For Internet Freedom,* Basic Books, 2012.

Maignien, Yannick. 'L'oeuvre d'art à l'époque de sa reproduction numérisée', Bulletin des bibliothèques de France, Ecole Nationale Supérieure des Sciences de l'Information et des Bibliothèques (ENSSIB), 1996, http://archivesic.ccsd.cnrs.fr/sic_00000302.

Manovich, Lev. *The Language of New Media,* Cambridge, Mass.: MIT Press, 2002.

Marvin, Carolyn. *When Old Technologies Were New: Thinking about Electric Communication in the Late Nineteenth Century,* New York, Oxford: Oxford University Press, 1990.

Mathias, Paul. 'De la dychtologie', in Eric Guichard (ed.) *Regards croisés sur l'internet,* Lyon: ENSSIB, 2011.

Melançon, Benoît. 'Sommes-nous les premiers lecteurs de l'Encyclopédie?', in Jean-Michel Salaün et Christian Vandendorpe (eds) *Les Défis de la publication sur le Web : hyperlectures, cybertextes et méta-éditions,* pp. 145-65. Lyon: ENSSIB, 2004.

Merleau-Ponty, Maurice. *Phénoménologie de la perception,* Paris: Gallimard, 1945; *Phenomenology of Perception,* Boston, Mass.: Routledge & Kegan Paul, 1962.

Merton, Robert. 'The Matthew Effect in Science', *Science* 159, no. 3810 (1968): 56-63.

Merzeau, Louise. 'Éditorialisation collaborative d'un événement', in *Communication & Organisation* 43, 1 (2014): 105-122.

Mongin, Olivier. *La condition urbaine: la ville à l'heure de la mondialisation,* Paris: Éditions du Seuil, 2007.

Monjour, Servanne. 'Dibutade 2.0: la "femme-auteur" à l'ère du numérique', *Sens public,* 24 September 2015, http://sens-public.org/article1164.html.

_____. 'La littérature à l'ère photographique: mutations, novations et enjeux (de l'argentique au numérique)', Ph.D. Thesis, Université de Montréal, 2015.

Morozov, Evgeny. 'The Meme Hustler', *The Baffler*, April 2103, http://thebaffler.com/salvos/the-meme-hustler.

Morozov, Evgeny. *The Net Delusion: The Dark Side of Internet Freedom*, New York: PublicAffairs, 2012.

_____. *To Save Everything, Click Here: The Folly of Technological Solutionism*, New York: PublicAffairs, 2013.

Morrison, Aimée. '"What's on Your Mind?": The Coaxing Affordances of Facebook's Status Update', in Julie Rak and Anna Poletti (eds) *Identity Technologies: Producing Online Selves*, Madison, Wisconsin: University of Winsconsin Press, 2013.

Nelson, T.H. 'Complex Information Processing: A File Structure for the Complex, the Changing and the Indeterminate', in *Proceedings of the 1965 20th National Conference*, ACM '65, New York: ACM, 1965, doi:10.1145/800197.806036.

Norman, Donald A. *The Design of Everyday Things*, New York: Basic Books, 2002.

O'Donnell, Daniel Paul. 'A "Thought Piece" on Digital Space as Simulation and the Loss of the Original', *dpod blog*, 11 February 2015, http://dpod.kakelbont.ca/2015/02/11/a-thought-piece-on-digital-space-as-simulation-and-the-loss-of-the-original/.

O'Neil, Mathieu. *Cyberchiefs: Autonomy and Authority in Online Tribes*, London, New York: Pluto Press, 2009.

Ostrom, Elinor. *Governing the Commons: The Evolution of Institutions for Collective Action, Cambridge*, United Kingdom: Cambridge University Press, 2015.

Preciado, Beatriz. *Pornotopia: An Essay on Playboy's Architecture and Biopolitics*, New York: Zone Books, 2014; *Pornotopie. Playboy et l'invention de la sexualité multimédia*, Paris: Flammarion, 2011.

Richards, Neil. *Intellectual Privacy: Rethinking Civil Liberties in the Digital Age*, Oxford: Oxford University Press, 2014.

Rose, Mark. *Authors and Owners: The Invention of Copyright*, Cambridge, Mass.: Harvard University Press, 1993.

Ruffel, Lionel. 'The Public Spaces of Contemporary Literature', *Qui Parle: Critical Humanities and Social Sciences 22:2* (21 March 2014): 101-22.

Sassen, Saskia. *Losing Control?: Sovereignty in the Age of Globalization*, New York: Columbia University Press, 2014.

_____. *Territory, Authority, Rights: From Medieval to Global Assemblages*, Princeton, N.J.: Princeton University Press, 2008.

_____. 'Who Owns our Cities – And why this Urban Takeover Should Concern Us all', *The Guardian*, 24 November 2015, http://www.theguardian.com/cities/2015/nov/24/who-owns-our-cities-and-why-this-urban-takeover-should-concern-us-all.

Schechner, Richard. *Performance Theory*, London: Routledge, 2009.

Schmitt, Carl. *Land and Sea*. Washington, DC: Plutarch Press, 1997.

Schmitt, Carl and G.L. Ulmen. *The Nomos of the Earth in the International Law of the Jus Publicum Europaeum*, New York: Telos Press, 2006.

Schnapp, Jeffrey. 'Knowledge Design', 2011, http://jeffreyschnapp.com/wp-content/uploads/2011/06/HH_lectures_Schnapp_01.pdf.

Schroeder, Ralph. *Rethinking Science, Technology, and Social Change*, Stanford: Stanford University Press, 2007.

Searle, John R. *The Construction of Social Reality*, New York: Free Press, 1997.

Seckin, Gul. 'Health Information on the Web and Consumers' Perspectives on Health Professionals' Responses to Information Exchange', *Medicine 2.0* 3, no. 2 (2014), doi:10.2196/med20.3213.

Serres, Michel. *Atlas*, Paris: Julliard, 1994.

Shirky, Clay. 'Shirky: Power Laws, Weblogs, and Inequality', 8 February 2003, http://www.shirky.com/writings/powerlaw_weblog.html.

Sloane, Sarah. *Digital Fictions: Storytelling in a Material World*, Stamford, Conn.: Ablex Pub., 2000.

Solove, Daniel J. *The Digital Person: Technology and Privacy in the Information Age*, New York: New York University Press, 2004.

Stallman, Richard. 'Why Open Source Misses the Point of Free Software', https://www.gnu.org/philosophy/open-source-misses-the-point.html.

Stern, Niels, Jean-Claude Guédon, and Thomas Wiben Jensen. 'Crystals of Knowledge Production: An Intercontinental Conversation about Open Science and the Humanities', *Nordic Perspectives on Open Science 1* (2015): 1, doi:10.7557/11.3619.

Striphas, T. 'Algorithmic Culture', *European Journal of Cultural Studies 18*, no. 4-5 (2015): 395-412, doi:10.1177/1367549415577392.

Stross, Randall. *Planet Google: One Company's Audacious Plan to Organize Everything We Know*, London: Simon and Schuster, 2009.

Suber, Peter. *Open Access*, Cambridge, Mass.: MIT Press, 2012.

Svensson, Patrik. 'Envisioning the Digital Humanities', *digital humanities quarterly 6*, no. 1 (2012), http://www.digitalhumanities.org/dhq/vol/6/1/000112/000112.html.

Valluy, Jérome. '"Editorialisation" (recherche bibliographique, Avril 2015)', *Terra-HN*, 2015, http://www.reseau-terra.eu/article1333.html.

Vandendorpe, Christian. *Du papyrus à l'hypertexte: essai sur les mutations du texte et de la lecture*, Paris: La Découverte, 1999, http://vandendorpe.org/papyrus/PapyrusenLigne.pdf.

Vial, Stéphane. *L'être et l'écran comment le numérique change la perception*, Paris: Presses universitaires de France, 2013.

Vincent-Lamarre, Philippe, Jade Boivin, Yassine Gargouri, Vincent Larivière, and Stevan Harnad. 'Estimating Open Access Mandate Effectiveness: The MELIBEA Score', in *Journal of the Association for Information Science and Technology (JASIST)* 67 (2016), http://eprints.soton.ac.uk/370203/.

Vitali-Rosati, Marcello. *Corps et virtuel : itinéraires à partir de Merleau-Ponty*, Paris: L'Harmattan, 2009.

_____. 'Digital Paratext: Editorialization and the Very Death of the Author', in Nadine Desrochers and Daniel Apollon (eds) *Examining Paratextual Theory and Its Applications in Digital Culture*, IGI Global, 2014, http://www.igi-global.com/book/examining-paratextual-theory-its-applications/97342.

_____. *Égarements: amour, mort et identités numériques*, Paris: Hermann, 2014, http://vitalirosati.com/liseuse/spip.php?rubrique3.

_____. 'Les algorithmes de l'amour', in *MuseMedusa*, no. 2 (2014), http://musemedusa.com/dossier_2/marcello_vitali-rosati/.

_____. 'Les revues littéraires en ligne: entre éditorialisation et réseaux d'intelligences', in *Études françaises 50*, no. 3 (2014): 83, doi:10.7202/1027191ar.

_____. 'Perceptibilité du virtuel et virtualisation de la perception', in *La transition du perçu à l'ère des communications*, Pessac: Presses universitaires de Bordeaux, 2013, pp. 191-206, http://www.lcdpu.fr/livre/?GCOI=27000100180410.

_____. *Riflessione e trascendenza: itinerari a partire da Levinas*, Pisa: ETS, 2003.

_____. *S'orienter dans le virtuel*, Paris: Hermann, 2012.

_____. 'Voir l'invisible: Gygès et la pornographie Facebook', *Sens-Public*, June 2012, http://sens-public.org/spip.php?article912.

_____. 'What Is Editorialization ?' *Sens public*, 4 January 2016, http://sens-public.org/article1059.html.

Warner, Michael. *The Letters of the Republic: Publication and the Public Sphere in Eighteenth-Century America*, Cambridge, Mass.: Harvard University Press, 1992.

Wiener, Norbert. *Cybernetics: Or Control and Communication in the Animal and the Machine,* New York: John Wiley & Sons, 1946.

Wormser, Gérard. 'Banco !... L'espace public à l'heure du numérique', *Sens Public*, 17 December 2010, http://www.sens-public.org/article800.html.